D1567800

NRA GUIDE TO THE BASICS OF PISTOL SHOOTING

Produced by the Education & Training Division
A Publication of the National Rifle Association of America

Eighth Printing

Second Edition—November 2009
©2009 The National Rifle Association of America

International Standard Book Number (ISBN): 978-0-935998-05-4

NR40830ES30600 10/14

DISCLAIMER

The NRA expressly disclaims any and all liabilities, losses, costs, claims, remands, suits or actions of any type or nature whatsoever, arising from or in any way related to: this manual; the use of this manual; any representation, drawing or statement made in this manual; or any claim that a particular action is in compliance or performed in accordance or pursuant to this manual.

This manual is under no circumstances to be viewed as a restatement of the law in any jurisdiction or to assure compliance with any applicable federal, state or local laws, ordinances, rules or regulations. You must consult a local attorney to ascertain compliance with all applicable federal, state or local laws, ordinances, rules or regulations and to advise you of the applicable duty of care required of firearms instructors in your jurisdiction.

Instructors should consult with their attorneys for advice on reducing their potential liability for injuries or damages which students or others may incur while learning to use pistols safely, or as a result of other activities. The effectiveness of theories of liability (e.g., strict liability, negligence and others) and methods for protecting oneself from liability (e.g., incorporation, waivers and others) vary between different jurisdictions, and the attorney consulted should be familiar with the law of the applicable jurisdiction.

Discharging firearms in poorly ventilated areas, cleaning firearms, or handling ammunition or lead-containing reloading components may result in exposure to lead. Have adequate ventilation at all times. Wash hands with water after exposure.

Great pains have been taken to make this book as complete as possible; however, it is designed to be used in conjunction with the classroom and firing range instruction of the NRA Basic Pistol Shooting Course. Reading this guide is not, in itself, sufficient to confer proficiency in pistol shooting, safety and maintenance. The reader of this book should obtain additional knowledge and hands-on training. Contact the NRA Education and Training Division at (703) 267-1500 for more information.

ACKNOWLEDGEMENTS

The NRA would like to acknowledge the efforts of those who participated in the development and production of this book:

Charles Mitchell, Manager, Training Department, Education & Training Division.

John Howard, National Manager, NRA Training Department, Education & Training Division and co-author of *NRA Guide to the Basics of Pistol Shooting*.

Stanton L. Wormley, Jr., NRA Certified Instructor and author of *NRA Guide to the Basics of Pistol Shooting*.

NRA Publications Division, which supplied a number of the drawings and photographs in *NRA Guide to the Basics of Pistol Shooting*.

Images for this book were also generously provided by the Boy Scouts of America, Kel-Tec CNC Industries, Inc., the National Firearms Museum, and Smith & Wesson. Some of the shooting accessories featured in photographs in this book were provided by Birchwood Casey, Brownells, Inc., Bushnell Outdoor Products, D.P.M.S. LLC, Hoppe's, Hornady Manufacturing Co., and MidwayUSA.

Credit is also due to the many NRA staff members who modeled for the photographs in *NRA Guide to the Basics of Pistol Shooting*, and to Andy Lander, John Howard, Teresa Howard, Chris Ray, John Stanley and Brian Zins for their contributions to the photographs for this book.

Additionally, the NRA would like to thank the many NRA Certified Instructors, NRA staff, NRA members, The NRA Foundation, and others whose assistance helped make this book possible.

TABLE OF CONTENTS

INTRODUCTION

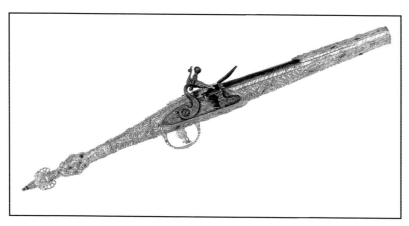

Turkish rat-tail flintlock pistol, from the collection of the National Fireams Museum.

The word *pistol* may have come from the name of a small town, Pistoia, in southern Italy, where handguns were manufactured in the 15th and 16th centuries. However, some scholars attribute its origin to the Russian word for a 15th-century matchlock gun: *pischol.* Other researchers believe that the word may derive from the Czechoslovakian word *pistala*, or pipe. Regardless of the true origin of the term, a common definition today for the word *pistol* is "a gun that has a short barrel and can be held, aimed and fired with one hand."

Many different types of pistols exist, including revolvers, semi-automatics, muzzleloaders, hinge-actions, bolt-actions and air pistols. Although the word *pistol* is frequently associated with semi-automatic handguns, it is proper to use *pistol* to refer to all types of handguns.

This book will deal primarily with the two types of pistols in most common use today: the revolver and the semi-automatic.

Although muzzleloading pistols are not covered in this book, the sport of shooting these unique guns has increased in popularity. To learn about these pistols, see the NRA publication *The Muzzleloading Pistol Handbook* (EZ 14350). See Appendix B, Information and Training Resources, for information on ordering NRA publications.

Air pistol shooting is also a very popular activity. This type of shooting can provide a wide variety of recreation and sport opportunities, from shooting in a basement or backyard range to competing in the Olympic Games. For information on air pistols, see the *NRA Neighborhood Airgun Program* booklet (EF 09181).

Americans own pistols today for many different reasons. Some people compete in the various types of pistol shooting matches held throughout the country, including those held at the collegiate and Olympic levels. Others own pistols for personal protection. Hunters, too, have found that the use of a pistol to take game can be a challenging and exciting experience, and nearly all of the 50 states allow pistol hunting.

A new shooter will quickly discover that pistol shooting is fun! It is a sport that requires good hand/eye coordination, mental concentration and discipline. The purpose of this book is to teach the safe and proper use of a pistol so that it can be enjoyed to the fullest extent.

The main focus of *The NRA Guide to the Basics of Pistol Shooting* is on helping the reader develop the knowledge, skills and attitude to safely and effectively handle and fire a pistol. Included are chapters on ammunition and pistol types; selecting ammunition, pistols and accessories; gun handling; shooting positions; and pistol shooting activities. These and other topics presented in this book form the core knowledge and skills used in all pistol shooting activities, from informal recreational shooting through hunting, competition and self-defense.

Although this book has a wealth of information on many aspects of pistol use, it is meant to be used within the framework of the NRA Basic Pistol Shooting Course, a hands-on program encompassing eight hours of classroom and range instruction. It is also used to support the NRA *FIRST Steps* Course. You should understand that merely reading a book—any book—will not, in and of itself, make you proficient in handling and using a pistol. For more information on the NRA Basic Pistol Shooting Course or any other NRA course, call (703) 267-1500.

A Gun Owner's Responsibilities

Americans enjoy a right that citizens of many other countries do not—the right to own firearms. But with this right come responsibilities. It is the gun owner's responsibility to store, operate and maintain his or her firearms safely. It is the gun owner's responsibility to ensure that unauthorized or untrained individuals cannot gain access to his or her firearms. And it is the gun owner's responsibility to learn and obey all applicable laws that pertain to the purchase, possession and use of a firearm in his or her locale. Guns are neither safe nor unsafe by themselves. When gun owners learn and practice responsible gun ownership, guns are safe.

SAFETY NOTE

The NRA's first and most fundamental Rule for Safe Gun Handling is **ALWAYS keep the gun pointed in a safe direction.** This rule must always be observed; it cannot be relaxed even for legitimate education or training purposes. Absolute, unvarying adherence to this most important of gun safety rules cannot be overemphasized.

In some of the photographs in this book that illustrate specific shooting stances or positions, it was sometimes necessary, for instructional purposes, to position the camera in front of the muzzle of the gun. At no time was an actual functioning firearm used in these photographs; special deactivated, non-firing training guns, or solid plastic gun simulators, were employed, and in some cases, the camera was fired by a remote trigger.

PART I

SAFETY

CHAPTER 1

BASIC FIREARM SAFETY

Safety is fundamental to all shooting activities. Whether you're practicing at the range, hunting in the field, or cleaning your gun in your workshop, the rules of firearm safety always apply.

Safe gun handling involves the development of *knowledge, skills* and *attitude*—knowledge of the gun safety rules, the skill to apply these rules, and a safety-first attitude that arises from a sense of responsibility and an understanding of potential dangers.

Most gun accidents are caused by *ignorance* and/or *carelessness*. Ignorance is a lack of knowledge—a person who handles a gun without knowing the gun safety rules or how to operate the gun is exhibiting a dangerous lack of knowledge. Equally dangerous is the person who, although knowing the gun safety rules and how to properly operate a gun, becomes careless in properly applying this knowledge. In both of these cases, accidents can easily happen. But when people practice responsible ownership and use of guns, accidents *don't* happen.

Though there are many specific principles of safe firearm operation, all are derived from just three basic safe gun handling rules.

FUNDAMENTAL RULES
FOR SAFE GUN HANDLING

ALWAYS keep the gun pointed in a safe direction.

ALWAYS keep the gun pointed in a safe direction. This is the primary rule of gun safety. A safe direction means that the gun is pointed so that even if it were to go off, it would not cause injury or damage. The key to this rule is to control where the muzzle or front end of the barrel is pointed at all times. Common sense dictates the safest direction, depending upon the circumstances. At the range, a "safe direction" is downrange. If only this one safety rule were always followed, there would be no injuries or damage from unintentional discharges.

ALWAYS keep your finger off the trigger until ready to shoot.

Keeping a firearm pointed in a safe direction is relatively easy with a long gun, such as a rifle or shotgun, as the longer barrel promotes muzzle awareness. The shorter length of the typical revolver or semi-automatic, and its ability to be held and fired in one hand, require that the shooter be even more conscious of where the gun is pointing.

ALWAYS keep your finger off the trigger until ready to shoot. Your trigger finger should always be kept straight, alongside the frame and out of the trigger guard, until you have made the decision to shoot. Unintentional discharges can be caused when the trigger of a loaded gun is inadvertently pressed by a finger left in the trigger guard instead of being positioned straight along the side of the gun's frame.

ALWAYS keep the gun unloaded until ready to use. A firearm that is not being used should always be unloaded. For example, at the range, your firearm should be left unloaded with the action open while you walk downrange to check your target. Similarly, a firearm that is stored in a gun safe or lock box should be unloaded (unless it is a personal protection firearm that may need to be accessed quickly for defensive purposes).

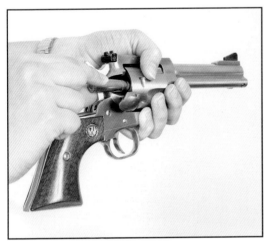

ALWAYS keep the gun unloaded until ready to use.

As a general rule, whenever you pick up a gun, point it in a safe direction with your finger off the trigger, engage the safety (if the gun is equipped with one), remove the magazine (if the gun is equipped with a removable magazine), open the action and visually and physically inspect the chamber(s) to determine if the gun is loaded or not. Unless the firearm is being kept in a state of readiness for personal protection, it should be unloaded. If you do not know how to open the action or inspect the firearm, leave the gun alone and get help from someone who does. Further information on pistol mechanisms will be presented in Part II: Pistol Mechanisms and Operation.

RULES FOR USING OR STORING A GUN

In addition to these three fundamental Rules for Safe Gun Handling, you need to observe a number of additional rules when you use or store your firearm.

Know your target and what is beyond. Whether you are at the range, in the woods, or in a self-defense situation, if you're going to shoot you must know what lies beyond your target. In almost all cases, you must be sure that there is something that will serve as a backstop to capture bullets that miss or go through the target. Even in an emergency, you must never

Semi-automatic pistols in particular can have many different safety and operating mechanisms, reflected in the variety of levers and controls found on various models.

fire in a direction in which there are innocent people or any other potential for mishap. Think first, shoot second.

Know how to use the gun safely. Before handling a gun, learn how it operates. Read the owner's manual for your gun. Contact the gun's manufacturer for an owner's manual if you do not have one. Know your gun's basic parts, how to safely open and close the action, and how to remove ammunition from the gun. No matter how much you know about guns, you must always take the time to learn the proper way to operate any new or unfamiliar firearm. Never assume that because one gun resembles another, they both operate similarly. Also, remember that a gun's mechanical safety is never foolproof. Guidance in safe gun operation should be obtained from the owner's manual or a qualified firearm instructor or gunsmith.

Knowing how to use the gun safely is especially important with pistols, as there is a multitude of different types of pistol mechanisms, each with its own specific operating procedure. Most long guns of a particular type (such as bolt-action rifles or pump-action shotguns) work in essentially the same way, allowing an individual familiar with one model to be likely to know how to operate another of the same type. This cannot always be said of pistols, particularly semi-automatic pistols.

Be sure your gun is safe to operate. Just like other tools, guns need regular maintenance. Proper cleaning and storage are a part of the gun's general upkeep. If there is any question regarding a gun's ability to function, it should be examined by a knowledgeable gunsmith. Proper maintenance procedures are found in your owner's manual.

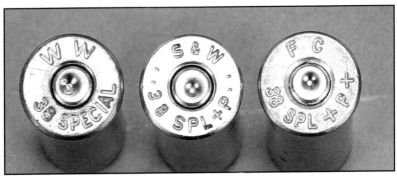

Some pistol cartridges come in loads that have the same external dimensions but operate at different pressure levels. The gun owner must know which of these loads are safe to fire in his or her gun.

Use only the correct ammunition for your gun. Each firearm is intended for use with a specific cartridge. Only cartridges designed for a particular gun can be fired safely in that gun. Most guns have the ammunition type stamped on the barrel and/or slide. The owner's manual will also list the cartridge or cartridges appropriate for your gun. Ammunition can be identified by information printed on the cartridge box and usually stamped on the cartridge head. Do not shoot the gun unless you absolutely know you have the proper ammunition.

Using only the correct ammunition for your gun is of special importance with pistols, as there are some pistol cartridges that have several names. Moreover, there are a number of different cartridges which have the same external dimensions, and thus fit in the same firearm chamber, but produce strikingly different operating pressures. Furthermore, even for the same cartridge there may be loadings having varying levels of pressure and performance. These higher-pressure loads must be used only in a firearm designed for them.

Eye and ear protection.

Wear eye and ear protection as appropriate. The sound of a gunshot can damage unprotected ears. Gun discharges can also emit debris and hot gas that could cause eye injury. Thus, both ear and eye protection are highly recommended whenever you are firing live ammunition in your gun. Safety glasses and ear plugs or muffs should also be worn by any spectators or shooting partners present during live-fire sessions.

Never use alcohol or drugs before or while shooting. Alcohol and many drugs can impair normal mental and physical bodily functions, sharply diminishing your ability to use a gun safely. These substances must never be used before or while handling or shooting guns.

Note that these effects are produced not just by illegal or prescription drugs. Many over-the-counter medications also have considerable side effects which may be multiplied when certain drugs are taken together or with alcohol. Read the label of any medication you take, even common non-prescription medications, or consult your physician or pharmacist for possible side effects. If the label advises against driving or operating equipment while taking the medication, you should also avoid using a firearm while taking it.

Store guns so they are inaccessible to unauthorized persons. It is your responsibility as a gun owner to take reasonable steps to prevent unauthorized persons (especially children) from handling or otherwise having access to your firearms. You have a number of options for accomplishing this, which are discussed in greater detail in Chapter 2: Safe Firearm Storage. The particular storage method you choose will be based upon your own particular home situation and security needs.

Be aware that certain types of guns and many shooting activities require additional safety precautions. There are many different types of firearms, some of which require additional safety rules or procedures for proper operation. These are commonly found in your firearm's owner's manual. Also, most sport shooting activities have developed sets of rules to ensure safety during competition. These rules are generally sport-specific; the procedures for loading your firearm and commencing fire, for example, are different in NRA bullseye shooting than in NRA Action Pistol competition (see Chapter 17: Pistol Shooting Activities and Opportunities for Skill Development).

SPECIAL RESPONSIBILITIES FOR PARENTS

Parents should be aware that a child could discover a gun when a responsible adult is not present. This situation could occur in the child's own home, the home of a neighbor, friend or relative, or in a public place (such as a park). To avoid the possibility of an accident in such a situation, the child should be taught to apply the following gun safety rules:

> **If you see a gun:**
> **STOP!**
> **DON'T TOUCH.**
> **LEAVE THE AREA.**
> **TELL AN ADULT.**

These four rules are part of a special accident-prevention program known as the Eddie Eagle GunSafe® Program. Developed by the NRA for young children (pre-kindergarden through third grade), it uses the friendly character of Eddie Eagle to teach children to follow Eddie's four rules.

CHAPTER 2

SAFE FIREARM STORAGE

Safe gun storage is an integral part of gun safety, and one of your prime responsibilities as a gun owner. By storing your guns safely, you not only avoid the possibility of an accidental shooting involving a child or other untrained person; you may also prevent a criminal from using your firearm against an innocent person. In addition, some jurisdictions have laws mandating secure firearm storage, and almost all jurisdictions have criminal negligence laws that can be applied to gun owners who do not take reasonable precautions in storing their firearms. A gun owner may also be liable to a civil lawsuit in the event that his or her unsecured gun is stolen and subsequently used during the commission of a crime.

Any firearm storage method chosen must provide an adequate level of protection to prevent unauthorized persons from accessing the guns. The determination of what is "adequate protection" is a matter of judgment on the part of the gun owner, and will vary with the situation. Also, the storage method or device used must allow any gun used for self-defense to be retrieved as needed to repel an intruder or an attack. Be aware that storage methods that provide a high level of security often do not allow quick and easy firearm access. Additionally, a gun storage device should provide some level of concealment. A gun that is not seen is less likely to be stolen. Concealment is achieved by storing the gun in a location or a device where it is hidden.

There is no one best method of gun storage nor one best type of locking or storage device. Each has advantages and limitations. You must choose the firearm storage method that is best for you, given your circumstances and preferences. It is also incumbent upon you as a responsible, law-abiding gun owner to know and observe all applicable state and local laws regarding safe gun storage.

TYPES OF LOCKING MECHANISMS

All storage methods designed to prevent unauthorized access utilize some sort of locking mechanism. Different types of locking mechanisms offer varying degrees of security and accessibility.

Keyed locks, such as padlocks and the lockable drawers of desks and nightstands, can offer a certain level of security (depending upon the construction of the lock and the storage device). However, under stress or in darkness it may be difficult for some to locate the correct key or to manipulate it in the lock.

Combination locks are often found on gun storage boxes, and range from simple triple-rotary-tumbler models to units that rival the mechanisms found on bank vaults. For many people, combination locks are both secure and familiar to use. Under stress, however, lock combinations can be confused or forgotten by the gun owner, and the tumblers can be challenging to manipulate quickly and accurately. Also, in darkness or dim light, combination locks can be virtually impossible to operate.

Simplex®-type locks provide a good combination of security and quick access. Such locks feature a number of buttons that are pushed in a specific order to open the device. With only minimal practice, these locks can be easily worked in total darkness. Locks having Simplex®-type mechanisms can be just as strong and tamper-resistant as any other.

Simplex®-type locking device.

Another advantage of a Simplex® lock is that incorrect entry blocks any further attempt to open the lock. A separate clearing code must be entered before the lock will accept the correct combination, making this lock even more resistant to unauthorized attempts to open it.

The basic Simplex®-type lock is a mechanical lock, and thus does not depend upon house current or batteries. Some locking devices combine Simplex® principles with modern electronics. Typically, such a storage device features a numeric keypad whose numbered buttons are pushed in a specific order to unlock.

A variation on this involves five *fingerpads*, ergonomically placed on the top or front of the device, which can easily be felt in the dark and which are pressed in a sequence (such as thumb, middle finger, little finger, ring finger) to open the device. Such locking mechanisms are often disabled when electric power is lost (as from dead batteries or a failure in house current). There usually is a provision for opening the box with a key under such circumstances, but this could be problematic under stress or in the dark. Some units that use house current have provisions for a backup battery power supply to ensure continuous operation.

A new type of gun storage device uses *biometrics* to control access. The most common type of this device features a computer-controlled fingerprint reader to activate unlocking. Though this technology is promising, there are still issues to be resolved regarding reliability of the reader to distinguish a fingerprint under a wide variety of circumstances.

Fingerpad-type locking device. Key provides manual override.

TYPES OF STORAGE DEVICES

There are many different methods for storing firearms safely inside and outside the home.

Gun cases are commonly used for the transportation and storage of firearms. Gun cases are typically of synthetic material, though some more costly models are made of aluminum. Some have integral locks; others feature hasps for small keyed or combination padlocks.

Gun cases can be used to transport a gun by air or other common carrier, or in a vehicle. Note that Federal law mandates that a gun transported across state lines in your vehicle must be in a "locked container" (such as a gun case) when it cannot be transported in a compartment

Plastic gun case secured with padlock.

separate from the driver's compartment, and some states also have additional requirements for transporting guns within their boundaries. In the home, gun cases serve to protect firearms from dust and moisture.

A *pistol lockbox* allows you to store a gun so that it is protected from unauthorized access but can still be retrieved quickly. Typically, such boxes are made of steel (thus offering more security than plastic gun cases) and feature integral keyed, combination or Simplex®-type locks. A few have electronic numeric keypads or fingerpads for quick access.

Gun safes are designed to offer the greatest level of security for your guns. Upper-end models provide walls and doors that are virtually impossible to defeat by brute force, high-security mechanical or electronic locks, and complex locking patterns that fasten the door to the frame in multiple

Gun safe.

locations with thick, hardened steel pins. Most of these models are too heavy and bulky for thieves to carry away easily, even when they are not bolted to the floor; some also offer a degree of fire protection.

Although appropriate for permanent firearm storage, gun safes may not be the best choice for the temporary storage of guns that may need to be quickly retrieved, as their opening procedure is often lengthy and noisy. Also, they provide little concealment value. No matter where a gun safe is put, almost anyone seeing it will recognize it as a device for the storage of firearms or other valuable items, making it a target for thieves and burglars.

Alternatively, a gun may be stored in a *lockable drawer* of a desk, nightstand, file cabinet or the like. Since it is easy for a gun owner to forget to lock such devices, and also since they may be easily forced open, the decision to store a gun in this manner must be reached only after a careful consideration of the circumstances, needs and risks involved.

Another alternative form of storage is a *lockable gun rack* allowing firearms (particularly long guns) to be displayed or stored openly. Since these devices do not offer either concealment or protection from moisture, dust, or fingerprints, they are best mounted in a locked gun closet or safe.

STORING A GUN SAFELY IN THE HOME

There are two types of home gun storage, each with benefits and limitations. *Long-term gun storage* involves the extended storage of firearms in a device offering a high degree of protection from theft and sometimes fire and moisture, but often at the expense of delayed access to the firearm. A gun safe is typically used for permanent firearm storage; its size and weight prevent easy theft, and its enclosed environment affords the best possible protection from fire damage, high humidity, and so forth.

Temporary or *quick-access gun storage methods* do not provide the same degree of protection as long-term storage methods, but allow easier gun availability when necessary. Some temporary gun storage methods are as simple as putting a gun in an unlocked kitchen or nightstand drawer. However, such measures do not prevent unauthorized persons from accessing the gun when the gun owner is not in the room. As a general rule, you should avoid storing a gun (loaded or otherwise) in an unlocked drawer, cabinet, etc. when you are not physically present in the home. Even when you *are* physically present, gun storage in unlocked areas may not be appropriate if you have children, relatives, friends or others around. You must balance the need for quick access against the need for safety. Greater security can be achieved by using a fingerpad-activated lockbox located by the bed or in the office, basement or TV room.

A few gun safes attempt to provide the best of both worlds by offering, in addition to the heavily-locked main firearm compartment, an auxiliary easy-access compartment containing a single pistol. Access to the auxiliary compartment is by a fingerpad that can be worked quickly, even in the dark. This combination long-term and easy-access storage device can work well if the gun safe is placed in the bedroom or other location in which fast access is most likely needed. When situated in a relatively inaccessible part of a home, however, the benefit of such a device is greatly diminished.

PART II

PISTOL MECHANISMS AND OPERATION

CHAPTER 3

INTRODUCTION TO PISTOL MECHANISMS

All firearms fundamentally take the form of a tube (known as the *barrel*) that is closed at one end, and into which are put a chemical propellant (*gunpowder*) and, on top of that, a snug-fitting projectile (*bullet*). When the gunpowder is ignited, hot, high pressure gas is created, which forces the projectile out of the open end of the barrel at high speed. Early firearms were *muzzle-loading*: the gunpowder and then the projectile were put into the barrel from the open or *muzzle* end of the barrel. In modern

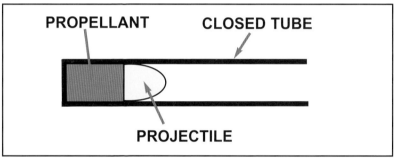

Simplified schematic of basic firearm design: a closed tube (barrel) with propellant (gunpowder) and a projectile (bullet). When the propellant is ignited, it generates high-pressure gas that forces the projectile out the open end (muzzle) at high speed.

rifles and pistols, however, the powder and bullet are combined into a single unit, the *metallic cartridge*, which also incorporates a pressure-sensitive component (*primer* or *priming compound*) that, when forcefully struck, ignites the powder (see Chapter 8: Ammunition Fundamentals).

All pistols that fire metallic cartridges are *breech-loading firearms*. A breech-loading firearm is one in which the cartridge is loaded into the rear of the barrel, or *breech*. Breech-loading fireams thus incorporate some method for both opening the breech, for cartridge loading, as well as for closing or locking the breech, to prevent the escape of the hot, high-pressure propellant gas that accelerates the bullet down the bore when the cartridge is fired.

Major components of breech-loading pistols include the *frame*, the *barrel,* and the *action*. The *action* determines how the gun operates, and is simply *the collection of parts that serve to fire the gun*. Action components are involved in loading a cartridge, closing and/or locking the breech,

Pistols have many types of actions. Clockwise from top left: single-action semi-automatic, double-action semi-automatic, double-action revolver, and single-action revolver.

cocking the *hammer* or *striker* (the parts that cause the firing pin to ignite the cartridge), and extracting and/or ejecting the fired case. The *frame* is the component in which all the action parts are housed, and to which the barrel is connected.

PISTOL COMPONENTS

All pistols share a number of similar components, including a *trigger mechanism* that releases a spring-powered *hammer* or *striker* to fire the cartridge. (Technically, cartridge ignition occurs as a result of the strike of the *firing pin*, which may be integral with the hammer or striker, or a separate piece that is pushed forward by the hammer or striker). Virtually all pistol actions have one or more *safety mechanisms.* In addition, specific action types have a variety of components to close and/or lock the breech: a *slide* in semi-automatic pistols, a *bolt* in bolt-action pistols, and so on. In revolvers, the breech is closed not by a separate component, but by a part of the frame called the *recoil shield.*

Revolver actions also include the *cylinder*, which has *chambers* that hold the cartridges, as well as the mechanism used for cylinder rotation.

Frame. The central component of most pistols is the *frame*, which contains the action parts, and to which are attached the stocks or grips and the barrel or barrels. Modern pistol frames are made of steel, aluminum, titanium and, ever more frequently, polymer materials.

Barrel. The *barrel* is a tube through which the bullet is propelled. In pistols, this is usually made of steel, and the hole through the tube, the *bore*, has spiral *rifling*, which spins the bullet for stability and accuracy. Rifling is formed by creating shallow *grooves* in the bore surface; the slightly raised areas between the grooves are called the *lands*. At the rear, the bore enlarges to form the *chamber*, which accepts a particular cartridge. The forward end of the barrel is the *muzzle*. Most pistol barrels range from 2" to 15", but may be any length.

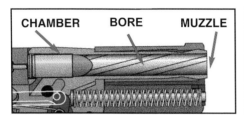 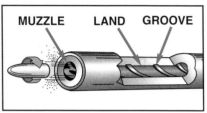

Left, cutaway of barrel (gray) showing chamber, bore with rifling, and muzzle. At right, detail of rifling in bore.

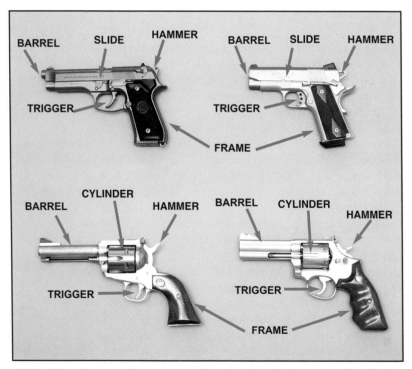

All pistols have the same major components: frame, barrel, and action parts such as the trigger, hammer, slide (semi-automatic pistols) and cylinder (revolvers).

Trigger. The *trigger* is a term used to denote both the entire mechanism that releases the part of the action (most commonly a *hammer* or *striker*) that causes the cartridge to be ignited, as well as the curved finger-piece that is pulled to fire.

With some firearms, such as single-action revolvers, the trigger directly releases the cocked hammer when it is pulled. In other types of trigger mechanisms, however, the trigger releases the spring-loaded hammer, firing pin or striker through an intermediary mechanism, such as a *sear* or *trigger bar*. Different action types have a variety of trigger mechanisms.

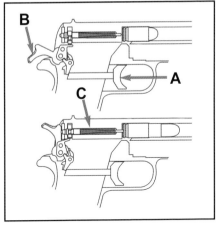

Depressing the trigger (A) activates components that release the hammer (B), which hits the firing pin (C), to fire the cartridge.

Safety Mechanisms. In general, firearm safeties can be *active* (the safety mechanism must be intentionally activated and deactivated by the shooter) or *passive* (the safety mechanism functions more or less automatically). Most commonly, active safety mechanisms take the form of a lever, sliding button, etc. that can manually be moved to a "safe" position to prevent firing, and a "fire" position to allow the gun to be discharged.

Passive safeties can take many forms, such as *grip safeties* that prevent firing unless the gun is properly gripped. Some other passive pistol safety mechanisms prevent the hammer from contacting the firing pin, or the firing pin from contacting the cartridge, unless the trigger has been pulled fully rearward.

Alternatively, many double-action semi-automatic pistols have *decocking mechanisms* instead of safeties. Decockers serve to drop the cocked hammer to the "down" position.

Remember, safeties are mechanical devices and can fail. Always follow the Fundamental Rules for Safe Gun Handling.

Breech Closing/Locking Mechanisms. In conventional semi-automatic pistols, the breech is closed and locked by a component called the *slide*, which rides on horizontal rails in the frame, and which has a flat vertical face which is positioned directly to the rear of the chamber, closing the breech. In some designs, the slide is locked to the barrel, resulting in a locked breech. Revolvers have no separate breech closing or locking mechanism. Instead, behind the cylinder is a flat face in the frame, the *recoil shield*, which supports the head of the cartridge in the chamber that is aligned with the firing pin and the barrel. Other pistol types have their own methods for closing or locking the breech.

TYPES OF PISTOL ACTIONS

The great majority of pistols that will be purchased for hunting, plinking, self-defense or target work will be of conventional revolver or semi-automatic pistol design. Revolver actions can be further subdivided into *single-action* and *double-action* types, while semi-automatic pistols are offered in a variety of different action designs, including *single-action, traditional double-action* and *double-action-only*. These action types will be discussed in detail in the following chapters.

For some hunting or target activities, pistols of other action types may be preferred. *Break-action pistols* consist of a frame that houses the action parts, and a barrel or barrels attached to the frame by way of a hinge pin or pivot pin. This design allows the action to be opened for loading or unloading by pivoting the barrel(s) downward or, less frequently, to the side. Most such guns have a manually-cocked external hammer. Because of their strength and accuracy, some break-action pistols are chambered for rifle cartridges and often have barrels 14" or longer.

A special category of the break-action pistol is the *derringer,* well-known to viewers of Western movies and TV shows. This is a light, small, short-barreled arm with one or two barrels, an external manual hammer, and a latch that releases the barrel to be pivoted downward or to the side. Derringers typically are chambered for pistol rounds.

Bolt-action pistols function in the same manner as bolt-action rifles. The *receiver* is usually tubular, with the *barrel* attached at its forward end. Inside the receiver is a *bolt* with protruding *locking lugs* that engage lug seats in the receiver. Turning the bolt both cocks the spring-loaded firing pin, and also rotates the locking lugs out of engagement, allowing the bolt to be pulled to the rear for extraction and loading. The receiver and barrel are mounted into a separate *mid- or rear-grip stock*.

Bolt-action pistols usually have long barrels and are most often chambered for rifle cartridges. Except for those used in target sports requiring iron sights, most bolt-action pistols are intended for long-range use, and thus are usually fitted with telescopic sights.

Additional pistol action types include *cannon-breech* and *multiple-barrel* systems. The operation of each type of pistol can be found in that gun's owner's manual.

FIREARM CYCLE OF OPERATION

Regardless of design, every firearm action must allow a strict sequence of events to take place. This sequence, known as the *cycle of operation,* consists of the following steps:

Firing: occurs when the trigger is pulled and the hammer or striker is released to fly forward, causing the firing pin to hit the primer or priming compound of the cartridge.

Unlocking: the initial step in the opening of the action. In locked-breech guns, this occurs when the bolt or breech block is unlocked from the barrel or receiver. In non-locked-breech guns, such as some semi-automatic pistols (see Chapter 5: Semi-Automatic Pistol Parts and Operation), the action is kept closed simply by the recoil spring, and opens only when chamber pressure overcomes slide inertia and spring pressure.

Extraction: the pulling of the spent cartridge case rearward out of the chamber, usually by a part called an *extractor.*

Ejection: the forcible throwing of the the spent case clear of the action by a component called the *ejector.*

Cocking: the movement of the hammer or firing pin to its rearward position, where it is retained against spring pressure by the trigger mechanism.

Feeding: the insertion of a live cartridge into the chamber.

Locking: the closing of the action (and, in locked-breech firearms, the engagement of the locking mechanism) so that the breech is sealed. After the *Locking* step, the cycle returns to the *Firing* step.

Not all guns go through every single step in the cycle above. For example, revolver mechanisms technically do not have a feeding step, as cartridges are manually inserted into the cylinder chambers.

CHAPTER 4

REVOLVER PARTS AND OPERATION

The primary feature of a revolver action is its rotating *cylinder.* Mounted on the frame just to the rear of the barrel, the cylinder contains several chambers for cartridges, each of which comes into alignment with the bore as the cylinder is rotated. The modern revolver action is an outgrowth of earlier designs, such as the *pepperbox,* which consisted of a drum containing a number of barrels, each with a live chambered round, that was manually rotated to bring each successive barrel into alignment with the hammer. Today, the term "revolver" universally refers to a type of pistol with a rotating cylinder.

TYPES OF REVOLVER MECHANISMS

There are generally two types of revolver actions: *single-action* and *double-action.* The single-action revolver is the older of the two designs, and

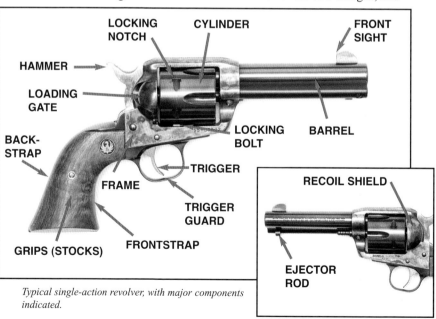

Typical single-action revolver, with major components indicated.

is so called because the pulling of the trigger performs but a single action: releasing the hammer. To operate a single-action revolver, the *hammer* is first manually cocked. This tensions the *mainspring* and retracts the *bolt* or *cylinder stop* out of engagement with one of the notches in the cylinder; freeing the cylinder to rotate. As the hammer is drawn further rearward, the *hand* (in Colt and Smith & Wesson terminology) or *pawl* (in Ruger nomenclature), which is attached to the hammer, moves vertically in a slot in the *recoil shield* of the frame, engaging an offset ratchet on the rear face of the cylinder and producing cylinder rotation. The ratchet and pawl are carefully designed so that, as the hammer is fully cocked and held rearward by the trigger, the cylinder is rotated only that amount required to bring the next chamber into alignment with the bore. At that point the bolt or cylinder stop snaps into the next notch, locking the cylinder in proper alignment. Pulling the trigger fires the revolver, and the cycle is repeated with the cocking of the hammer.

Double-action revolvers are so named because pulling the trigger both cocks and releases the hammer. Modern double-action revolvers can generally be fired in both the single- and double-action modes. The single-action mechanism of a double-action revolver is essentially identical to that of a single-action revolver, described above. The double-action mechanism is made possible by a separate *double-action sear* on the hammer that is

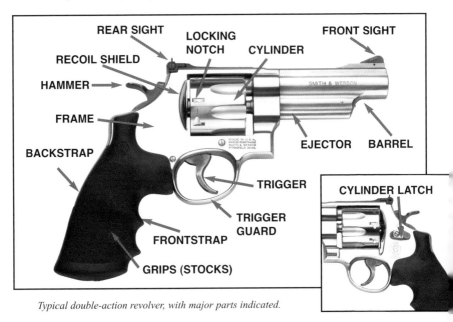

Typical double-action revolver, with major parts indicated.

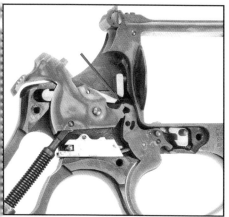
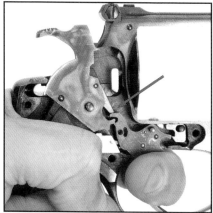

In the single-action mode (l.), the hammer is held back directly by the trigger (arrow). When the trigger is pulled, the hammer falls to fire the cartridge. This is the same for both single-action and double-action revolvers fired in the single-action mode. In the double-action mode (r.), the hammer is rotated rearward by the engagement of the tail of the trigger with the double-action sear on the hammer (arrow). When the trigger and hammer rotate through their full arc, the double-action sear slips off the trigger tail, firing the pistol.

engaged by the trigger such that rearward trigger movement first rotates the hammer to its cocked position, and then, with additional trigger movement, allows the hammer to fall, firing the revolver.

Although most double-action revolvers can be fired in the single-action mode, some models intended for personal protection are designed to allow double-action firing only, as this is generally considered

Revolvers are characterized by a rotating cylinder with several chambers. Each time the hammer is cocked (single-action revolver) or the trigger is pulled (double-action revolver) the hand or pawl rises in its window in the recoil shield (left, arrow) and engages one of the ratchets on the extractor star (right, arrow) of the cylinder, rotating it to the next chamber.

Most single-action revolvers are loaded through a gate in the frame (left). The cylinder of a modern double-action revolver (right) swings out to allow access to all chambers.

more practical in defensive situations. Some of these revolvers lack hammer spurs, or enclose a spurless hammer completely within the frame of the gun.

All revolvers must be manually loaded by inserting cartridges into the chambers of the cylinder, but variations exist on the way this is accomplished. With some of the oldest single-action revolver designs (as well as a very few modern small-size revolvers), loading sometimes requires removal of the cylinder, which is then filled with cartridges and reinstalled in the revolver. Most single-action revolvers, however, allow loading by way of a spring-loaded gate in the right side of the frame that, when opened, gives access to a single chamber of the cylinder. Loading is accomplished by inserting a fresh cartridge into each exposed chamber, one at a time. To unload the gun, an *ejector rod* is used to push empty cases out of the open loading gate. Some of these revolvers require that the hammer be set at the half-cock position before the cylinder can be rotated.

Faster loading and unloading was permitted by two later designs. *Top-break* revolvers, which originated in the latter part of the 1800s, feature a two-piece frame that is hinged forward of the cylinder, and a latch at the rear of the top strap (the portion of the frame directly above the cylinder). When the latch is disengaged, the barrel and the upper portion of the frame rotate forward, opening the action, exposing the chambers and (with most designs), extracting spent cases or live rounds from all chambers simultaneously. Loading is accomplished as with other revolvers, by inserting fresh cartridges into each chamber, one at a time.

The top-break revolver is an antiquated design that today has been superseded by the stronger *swing-out cylinder* design, which represents the pinnacle of revolver evolution to date. Instead of a hinged two-piece frame, such guns have a one-piece solid frame with a laterally-swinging *crane* (Colt and Ruger) or *yoke* (Smith & Wesson and Taurus), on which the cylinder and ejector rod are mounted. When the action is closed, the crane fits flush against the frame, and the cylinder is centered in the frame. The action is locked closed by various latch mechanisms, some of which engage the ejector rod at the front, the center pin at the rear (or both simultaneously), while there are other systems that lock the crane directly to the frame. A *cylinder release latch,* usually on the left side of the frame but sometimes on the crane, releases the crane so that the cylinder can be swung outward from the frame. In this open position, the ejector rod can be pushed to extract empty cases or live cartridges (or, if struck smartly enough, to eject cases or cartridges completely free of the cylinder).

Traditionally, for both proper functioning and extraction, revolver cartridges have been rimmed. However, some rimless semi-automatic cartridges can be fired in revolvers by the use of special devices known as *moon clips,* thin metal tabs with circular cutouts that snap around the extractor groove of a rimless cartridge. Moon clips provide purchase for the extractor star, and come in two-cartridge, three-cartridge (half-moon) and five- or six-cartridge (full-moon) varieties. All allow more rapid revolver reloading.

Revolvers are unique among conventional firearms in having a chamber that is separate from the barrel. This design also results in another unique feature: the *barrel-cylinder gap.* This gap, which is normally around 0.004"-.008", allows clearance between the face of the cylinder and the barrel for smooth cylinder rotation. Some gas also escapes from this gap— not enough to substantially lower velocities, but sufficient to be seen and heard, and to mark objects (or injure fingers) positioned close to this gap.

REVOLVER SAFETY MECHANISMS

In general, both single-action and double-action revolvers lack safeties of the type found on many other arms. Traditionally, it has been felt that the long, heavy pull of double-action revolvers, or the two-stage method of operation of single-action revolvers, made unintentional discharges extremely unlikely. Today, virtually all modern revolvers are produced with internal safety devices that require no deliberate shooter activation, and which are automatically disengaged when the trigger is properly pulled. However, many models include action locking mechanisms for storage.

Revolvers typically employ various types of passive safety mechanisms. As a general rule, these mechanisms work by preventing the hammer from contacting the firing pin unless the trigger is pulled fully rearward. (In revolvers in which the firing pin is part of the hammer, the safety mechanism prevents the hammer from falling fully forward unless the trigger is pulled.) These passive mechanisms help prevent an inadvertent discharge of a cocked revolver.

REVOLVER CYCLE OF OPERATION

Firing. With either single-action or double-action designs, a revolver is fired simply by pulling the trigger. While a single-action pull is usually short and relatively light, double-action pulls are long and fairly heavy.

Unlocking. With all revolver designs, as the hammer begins to move rearward, the bolt or cylinder stop retracts from its notch to allow cylinder rotation, bringing the next chamber into alignment with the bore.

Extraction and Ejection. With single-action designs that are loaded and unloaded through a loading gate, spent shells are extracted and/or ejected one at a time by manipulation of the ejector rod. With swing-out cylinder revolvers, the action must first be opened, normally by means of a latch on the left side of the frame or on the crane that is manipulated to allow the crane and cylinder to swing out. Once the cylinder is exposed, the shooter presses the ejector rod, which extracts (or, if worked with sufficient force, ejects) shells from the cylinder.

Feeding. With the empty chambers of the cylinder exposed (as with swing-out designs), or with the loading gate open (as with most single-action designs), cartridges are manually inserted into the chambers. After all chambers are full, the action is closed by swinging the cylinder shut or by closing the loading gate, depending upon the revolver design.

Cocking. Cocking is accomplished by manually retracting the hammer (in single-action designs) or by simply pulling the trigger (in double-action designs). Regardless of design, hammer cocking also brings each successive chamber of the cylinder into alignment with the bore.

Locking. With all revolver designs, the cylinder is locked into alignment with the bore by a bolt or cylinder stop, which enters a notch in the circumference of the cylinder.

CHAPTER 5

SEMI-AUTOMATIC PISTOL PARTS AND OPERATION

In general, semi-automatic firearms utilize the pressure generated by the ignition of the cartridge to perform the cycle of operation.

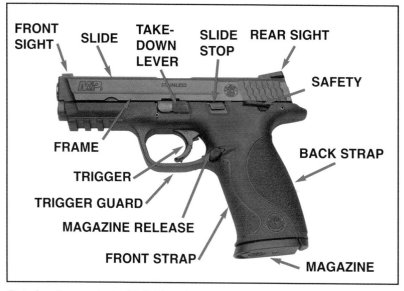

FRONT SIGHT · SLIDE · TAKE-DOWN LEVER · SLIDE STOP · REAR SIGHT · SAFETY · FRAME · TRIGGER · TRIGGER GUARD · MAGAZINE RELEASE · FRONT STRAP · BACK STRAP · MAGAZINE

Typical semi-automatic pistol, left side, with major parts indicated.

Semi-automatic pistols consist of a *frame*, on which is mounted a *slide* which can freely move in the fore-and-aft direction on rails in the frame. In some designs the barrel is fully contained within the slide, and in others it is rigidly attached to the frame, with the slide positioned to its rear. In both designs, a vertical face (*breech face*) on the slide abuts the chamber end of the barrel. On locked-breech designs (see below), the barrel locks to the slide by way of *lugs* that enter recesses in the slide, by the physical interference of a shoulder on the barrel with the rear edge of the ejection port of the slide, or other methods. The slide also houses the *firing pin* and *extractor*, while a fixed frame-mounted blade *ejector* is the most common means of ejection. An *ejection port* in the slide provides a means for empty shells to exit the action. Ignition is by either an *external hammer*, an *internal hammer*, or a spring-loaded *striker* or firing pin.

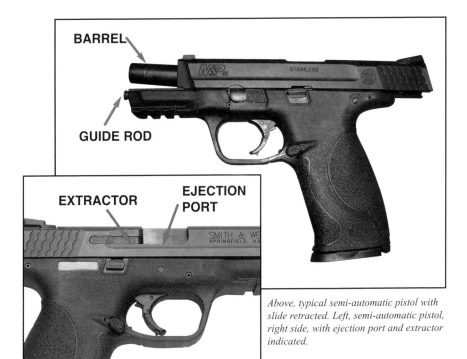

Above, typical semi-automatic pistol with slide retracted. Left, semi-automatic pistol, right side, with ejection port and extractor indicated.

TYPES OF SEMI-AUTOMATIC PISTOL MECHANISMS

There are generally three types of semi-automatic actions: *blowback-operated, recoil-operated,* and *gas-operated.*

Blowback-Operated Actions

In *blowback-operated* semi-automatic pistols, the action is not mechanically locked, and the weight of a heavy slide, plus a strong recoil spring, is all that keeps the action closed. Upon firing, chamber pressure created by cartridge ignition pushes the slide rearward, compressing the recoil spring. The inertia of the slide, aided by spring resistance, keeps the action closed long enough for pressure in the chamber and bore to drop to a safe level. Blowback designs are generally restricted to pistols firing low-powered cartridges (typically .22 LR, .25 ACP, .32 ACP and .380 Auto).

Recoil-Operated Actions

With *recoil-operated* semi-automatic pistol actions, when the action is closed, the barrel is locked to the slide. Upon firing, the barrel and slide recoil rearward together for a distance before the barrel unlocks and allows the slide to travel further rearward to complete the cycle.

Most self-loading pistols chambered for cartridges of the power of the 9 mm Para or greater use recoil-operated actions. There are many mechanical designs for both locking and unlocking the actions of such pistols.

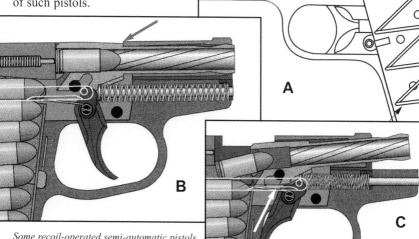

Some recoil-operated semi-automatic pistols lock to the slide by way of lugs on the barrel that fit into grooves in the slide (A, arrow). Alternatively, in many modern designs a shoulder on the chamber end of the barrel engages the edge of the ejection port in the slide (B, arrow) to lock the two parts together. Angled cam surface on barrel underlug (C, white arrow) engages crosspin in frame to lower the rear of the barrel out of lockup with the slide as the two parts recoil rearward together.

Gas-Operated Actions

In gas-operated actions, high-pressure propellant gas is bled from the bore through a small hole in the barrel. This, in turn, exerts pressure on a piston or other component, driving it rearward to unlock the breech and work the action.

SEMI-AUTOMATIC PISTOL MAGAZINES

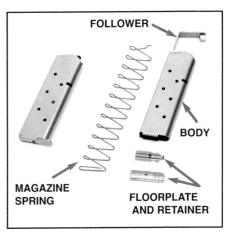

Most semi-automatic firearms utilize detachable *box magazines,* which afford one of the main advantages of such arms: rapid reloading. High-capacity magazines confer the additional benefit of being able to fire a large number of rounds in succession without reloading.

Box magazines typically have a steel, aluminum or plastic *body* which houses the

This pistol magazine consists of a magazine spring, follower, magazine body, floorplate and floorplate retainer. Some magazines have a welded floorplate.

cartridges and the magazine's internal components. At the bottom of the magazine is a *floorplate,* usually of the same material. This is often removable to allow magazine cleaning. Inside the magazine are the *magazine spring* and *follower*, which together push the cartridges in the magazine upward into position for reliable feeding.

SEMI-AUTOMATIC TRIGGER MECHANISMS

Modern semi-automatic pistols can achieve ignition by way of both external and internal hammers, or by a spring-powered striker or firing pin that is held to the rear by the sear or trigger bar. Semi-automatic pistols also incorporate some sort of *disconnector* mechanism, which requires that the trigger be released and then re-pressed each time a shot is fired. This prevents the gun from machine-gunning, or firing repeatedly, when the trigger is pulled and held back.

Single-Action and Double-Action Semi-automatic Trigger Systems

Contemporary semi-automatic pistols can be divided into categories by the manner in which their triggers operate.

Single-action semi-automatics require the hammer to be cocked manually for the first shot; the reciprocating slide cocks the hammer for all subsequent shots. Single-action semi-automatics offer the same short, crisp and relatively light trigger pull for the first shot and for all subsequent shots.

An alternative to the single-action semi-automatic is the *traditional double-action* pistol, which may also be described as a *double/single action*. In this type of mechanism, the first shot is fired with the hammer down, in the double-action mode—i.e., a long, relatively heavy trigger pull both cocks and releases the hammer—and subsequent shots are fired in the single-action mode. This allows the gun to be carried safely with a cartridge in the chamber and the hammer lowered, giving a rapid first shot.

Some pistol users—particularly among law enforcement—wanted the rapid reloading and increased firepower of the semi-automatic, combined with the long, heavy pull of the double-action revolver. This pull was considered to be less conducive to an unintentional discharge than the short, light pull of the single-action or traditional double-action pistol. This led to the development of *double-action only (DAO)* semi-automatics, which, as their name implies, require a long double-action pull for every shot.

In addition to the broad categories above, a number of other pistol types incorporate novel designs, many of which seek to combine the fast and accurate first shot capability afforded by a single-action trigger pull with the safety of hammer-down carry. Some of these pre-cock a hammer or internal striker, giving a "semi-double-action" pull for the first shot. A few designs can be fired in the both the single-action and traditional double-action modes, affording the gun owner a choice of trigger types.

SEMI-AUTOMATIC SAFETY MECHANISMS

Semi-automatic pistol safety systems can assume a dizzying variety of forms. Probably the most familiar are the pivoting thumb levers located on the frame or slide. These are sometimes located on the left side only; however, on many recent designs, they are located bilaterally for ambidextrous use. While many thumb safeties are pivoted downward to disengage, some work in the opposite direction. Such safeties mounted on the frame typically block the sear, while those mounted on the slide usually prevent the hammer from contacting the firing pin.

A different type of safety system found on some traditional double-action pistols is the *hammer drop safety*, also known as a *decocker*. When this is engaged, the hammer falls harmlessly to its lowered position. With any

Semi-automatic pistols feature a variety of different safety mechanisms, including (l. to r.) slide-mounted decockers, frame-mounted safeties, and trigger safeties.

pistol of this type, firing a shot, or simply working the slide to feed a round into the chamber, leaves the hammer in the cocked position. Since such pistols are not designed to be safely carried with a round in the chamber and the hammer back, the hammer must be lowered before the pistol is holstered, placed in a pistol box, etc. The decocking mechanism safely accomplishes this. Double-action-only (DAO) semiautomatic pistols may have a thumb safety or, alternately, no active safety mechanism at all.

All semi-automatic pistols normally exhibit one or more *passive safety systems*, such as an inertia firing pin, a magazine disconnect (which prevents firing the round in the chamber if the magazine is removed), grip safety, or passive firing pin block that prevents forward firing pin travel unless the trigger is depressed.

SEMI-AUTOMATIC CYCLE OF OPERATION

All semi-automatic pistols have essentially the same cycle of operation. However, some steps in the cycle may not apply to all action types. For example, double-action-only (DAO) semi-automatic pistols do not have a "cocking" step.

Firing. Pulling the trigger releases an internal or external hammer that strikes the firing pin and fires the cartridge, or it may release a cocked, spring-powered striker or firing pin in the slide.

Unlocking. The pattern of locking is determined by the nature of the semi-automatic mechanism. With recoil-operated actions, mechanical camming

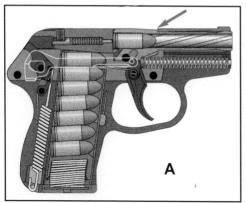

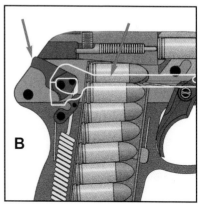

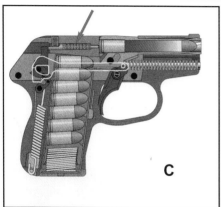

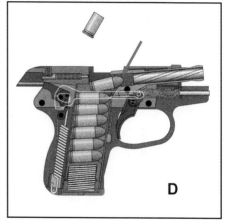

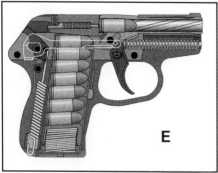

Semi-automatic cycle of operation, shown here with double-action-only pistol with a cartridge in the chamber and the hammer down in its ready position.(A). The barrel and slide are locked together by way of shoulder on chamber end of barrel (arrow). Pulling the trigger (B) causes the trigger bar (white outline, right arrow) to cock the hammer (left arrow). When the trigger rotates the hammer through its full arc, it falls, hitting the firing pin (arrow), firing the gun (C). As the slide recoils to the rear (D), the rear of the barrel drops down and unlocks from the slide, and the empty case is extracted and ejected. The slide quickly returns forward, and the breechface engages the top cartridge in the magazine, feeding it into the chamber (arrow). Finally, the slide returns fully forward, the fresh cartridge feeds fully into the chamber, the barrel and slide lock together, and the trigger bar resets (E).

surfaces serve to unlock the barrel from the slide after the two components have traveled rearward together a short distance. Gas-operated actions utilize gas pressure tapped from the bore to impel the slide rearward and unlock the action. Blowback-operated systems are by definition unlocked, so no unlocking is necessary. In such systems, the action opens simply when the gas pressure in the chamber and bore overcomes the forward force of the recoil spring and the inertia of the slide or bolt.

Extraction. A claw extractor mounted on the slide face engages the rim of the cartridge case and pulls it from the chamber after the action unlocks.

Ejection. As the slide moves smartly to the rear carrying a spent cartridge case, an ejector—usually a standing blade mounted in the frame—contacts the case head, throwing the case out of the action through the ejection port.

Cocking. At or near the extreme rearward limit of its travel, the reciprocating slide cocks the hammer or striker, which is held rearward against spring tension by the trigger mechanism.

Feeding. The compressed recoil spring pushes the slide rapidly forward, stripping a cartridge from the magazine and feeding it into the chamber.

Locking. With locked-breech semi-automatic designs, locking of the action occurs during the last fraction of an inch of forward motion of the slide. In the vast majority of designs, the rear of the barrel is cammed upward as it moves forward so that its locking surfaces engage the slide or frame, locking the action. With blowback-operated designs, no locking occurs; the momentum of the forward-moving bolt or slide is sufficient to fully chamber a cartridge and close the action (at which point the action is said to be *in battery*). Only the force of the compressed recoil spring, combined with the inertia of the bolt or slide, keeps the action closed.

CHAPTER 6

OPERATING DOUBLE-AND SINGLE-ACTION REVOLVERS

Gun handling consists of the processes to safely and efficiently load, fire, and unload the pistol. There are specific techniques for performing these functions with single- and double-action revolvers.

LOADING

Loading double-action and single-action revolvers involves two separate and very different procedures.

Loading Double-Action Revolvers

Almost all double-action revolvers feature a *swing-out cylinder* operated by a latch that, in most models, is located on the left side of the frame (see Chapter 4: Revolver Parts and Operation). With the revolver held in the right hand (for both right- and left-handed shooters), pointed in a safe direction with the trigger finger outside the trigger guard and alongside the frame, the cylinder latch is engaged with the right hand thumb. Note that a few revolver models locate the cylinder latch on the crane; engaging the latch must be done with the left hand.

With the cylinder latch disengaged, the left hand is placed around the frame and the left-hand fingertips push the cylinder out of the frame, to the left. The cylinder should never be swung out violently, as is sometimes seen in motion pictures; this causes damage to the revolver.

Once the cylinder is fully open, the revolver's muzzle is pointed slightly downward. With the revolver held in the left hand, live cartridges are inserted, one by one, into the chambers of the cylinder with the right hand. When the cylinder is full, the left-hand thumb pushes it fully back into the frame. A click will be heard when the cylinder is locked in place by the cylinder latch.

At this point, the revolver is ready to fire. A firing grip may be obtained with the right hand (for right-handed shooters) or the left hand (for left-handed shooters).

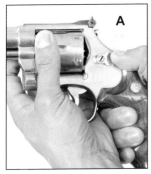
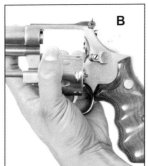
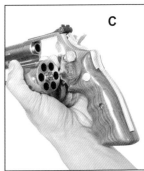

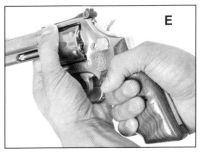

When beginning to load a double-action revolver, it should be held in the right hand and the cylinder latch operated by the right thumb (A). Once the cylinder latch is disengaged, the left hand is placed around the frame and the left-hand fingers push the cylinder to the left (B). This exposes all the chambers (C). The gun's muzzle is pointed slightly downward and live cartridges are inserted into the chambers, one by one (D). When the cylinder is full, it is swung back into the frame until it locks closed (E).

Loading Single-Action Revolvers

Instead of a cylinder that swings out, single-action revolvers usually have a right-side *loading gate* that is swung open to allow access to one chamber at a time.

For a right-handed shooter, the revolver is initially held in the right hand, the hammer put in the half-cock position (on some models), and the loading gate opened with the right-hand thumb. The gun is then transferred to the left hand and is turned slightly counterclockwise, with the muzzle pointed downward (but still in a safe direction). Next, the cylinder is rotated to expose an empty chamber. A fresh cartridge is inserted into the chamber with the right hand, and then the chamber is rotated to expose the next empty chamber. This process is repeated until all the chambers are full, at which point the loading gate is closed.

For left-handed shooters, the revolver is held in the left hand, the hammer is placed in the half-cock position if necessary, and the loading gate opened with the right-hand thumb. With the gun rotated slightly counterclockwise and held with the muzzle down (but still pointed in a safe direction), the cylinder is rotated with the right hand until an empty chamber is fully exposed, and a fresh cartridge inserted into it. The cylinder is rotated to expose the next empty chamber, and the loading process is repeated until all the chambers are full, at which point the loading gate is closed.

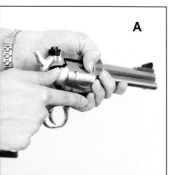

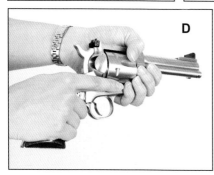

To load a single-action revolver (for a right-handed shooter), transfer the gun to the left hand and use the right thumb to engage the loading gate located on the right side of the frame (A). Open the gate and rotate the cylinder to expose an empty chamber (B). With some revolver designs, the hammer must be put in the half-cock position before the loading gate can be opened and the cylinder rotated. Insert a live cartridge into the empty chamber (C), and continue the process until the cylinder is full, at which point the loading gate is closed (D).

FIRING

Firing the revolver involves slightly different processes, depending upon whether a double- or single-action gun is used.

Firing Double-Action Revolvers

Almost all modern double-action revolvers can be fired in either of two modes: the double-action mode or the single-action mode.

In the double-action mode, the revolver is fired simply by pulling the trigger through its long double-action arc when it is pointed at the target. This action advances the cylinder, and both cocks the hammer and releases it when fully cocked, firing the cartridge. Pulling the trigger again advances the cylinder to the next chamber and cocks and releases the hammer, firing another cartridge. This procedure is repeated until the desired number of shots is fired, or all the cartridges are spent.

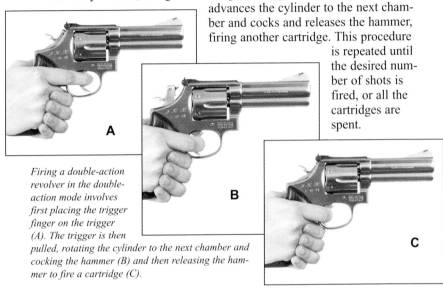

Firing a double-action revolver in the double-action mode involves first placing the trigger finger on the trigger (A). The trigger is then pulled, rotating the cylinder to the next chamber and cocking the hammer (B) and then releasing the hammer to fire a cartridge (C).

Most double-action revolvers can also be fired in the single-action mode. In this mode, with the gun pointed in a safe direction, the hammer is first cocked (either with the thumb of the firing hand in a one-hand shooting grip, or by the thumb of the support or non-firing hand, if a two-hand grip is employed). Cocking the hammer advances the cylinder to the next chamber. The revolver is then fired by simply pulling the trigger. To fire another shot, the hammer is again manually cocked, which advances the cylinder to the next chamber. This process of cocking and firing may be repeated until the desired number of shots is fired, or until all the cartridges in the cylinder are spent.

The shooter will notice a distinct difference in trigger pull quality and weight in these two modes. In the double-action mode, the trigger pull is long and relatively heavy--usually around eight to 15 pounds. In the single-action mode, in contrast, the trigger releases after a very short pull, usually at a light weight of only two or three pounds.

It is also worth noting that some double-action revolvers are designed to work only in the double-action mode. This is accomplished by such design features as shrouds or frames that enclose the hammer, hammers that lack a spur, or the elimination of the internal contact surfaces on the trigger or hammer that produce the single-action pull.

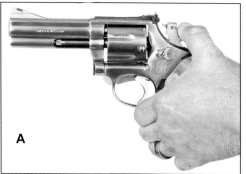

A

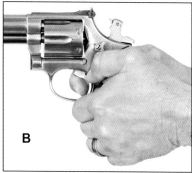

B

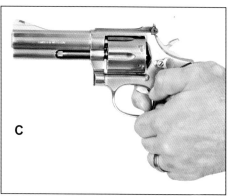

C

To fire a double-action revolver in the single-action mode, the hammer is cocked with the support-hand thumb (A) or firing-hand thumb. The gun is then aimed with the hammer in the fully cocked position (B). Firing is accomplished simply by pulling the trigger, which causes the hammer to fall and the firing pin to hit the cartridge primer, firing the revolver (C).

In both the double-action and single-action modes, the shooter must avoid grasping the revolver in such a way that puts the non-firing hand near the barrel/cylinder gap. Hot, high-pressure gas escaping through this gap could injure a finger carelessly placed close to it.

Firing Single-Action Revolvers

The process for firing single-action revolvers is identical to that for firing double-action revolvers in the single-action mode. With the revolver pointed in a safe direction, the hammer is first cocked (either with the thumb of the firing hand in a one-hand shooting grip, or by the thumb of the support or non-firing hand, if a two-hand grip is employed). Cocking the hammer advances the cylinder to the next chamber. The revolver is then fired by pulling the trigger. To fire another shot, the hammer must again be manually cocked, which once more advances the cylinder to the next chamber. This process of cocking and firing may be repeated until the desired number of shots is discharged, or the cartridges are all fired.

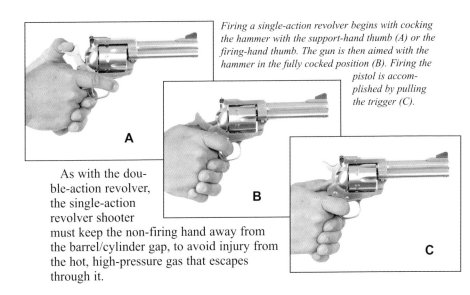

Firing a single-action revolver begins with cocking the hammer with the support-hand thumb (A) or the firing-hand thumb. The gun is then aimed with the hammer in the fully cocked position (B). Firing the pistol is accomplished by pulling the trigger (C).

A

B

C

As with the double-action revolver, the single-action revolver shooter must keep the non-firing hand away from the barrel/cylinder gap, to avoid injury from the hot, high-pressure gas that escapes through it.

DECOCKING

For a variety of reasons, it may become necessary for a shooter firing a single-action revolver, or a double-action revolver in single-action mode, to lower the hammer on a chamber containing a live cartridge.

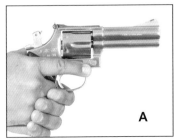
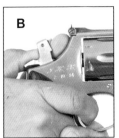
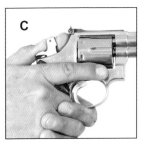

B

C

A

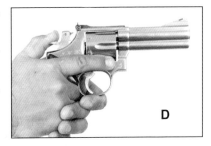

To decock a revolver, first put the trigger finger outside the trigger guard (A). Place the support hand thumb between the hammer and frame, engage the hammer spur with the firing-hand thumb, and pull the trigger (B). Take the finger off the trigger and ease the hammer forward until it touches the support-hand thumb (C). Remove the support-hand thumb and ease the hammer the rest of the way down (D).

D

To properly lower the cocked hammer of a revolver, first take the trigger finger off the trigger and put it outside the trigger guard, along the frame. Place the support-hand thumb in between the cocked hammer and the frame, and engage the hammer spur with the firing-hand thumb. Pull the trigger, being careful to control the released hammer with the firing-hand thumb. The placement of the support-hand thumb between the hammer and frame prevents the hammer from setting off the cartridge, if it slips.

When the hammer contacts the support-hand thumb, release the trigger and place the trigger finger outside the trigger guard, alongside the frame. Then, with the firing hand thumb still controlling the hammer, remove the support-hand thumb from between the hammer and frame, and ease the hammer the rest of the way down. The revolver may be unloaded or left loaded for future use.

UNLOADING

The mechanisms of double-action and single-action revolvers require unloading procedures that are very different.

Unloading Double-Action Revolvers

With the revolver held in the right hand, the trigger finger outside the trigger guard and the muzzle pointing in a safe direction, the right thumb disengages the cylinder latch (except in those models, discussed earlier, in which the latch is on the crane, which requires the use of the left hand). The fingers of the left hand encircle the frame and push the cylinder out of the frame, to the left. With the cylinder fully open the shooter may choose two methods of removing spent cases and live cartridges from the chambers. With the revolver's muzzle pointing slightly downward, the shooter may push rearward on the ejector rod, raising both the brass cases and live cartridges out of the cylinder. This allows them to be removed, one by one, from the chambers using the right hand (while the left hand supports the revolver).

Alternatively, the shooter may hold the gun in the left hand, with the cylinder open and the left-hand fingers through the opening in the frame that is normally occupied by the cylinder. The muzzle is then pointed straight up, and the left-hand thumb forcefully pushes the ejector rod downward. If hard extraction is encountered, the ejector rod may be hit sharply with the palm of the right hand. Either technique will have the effect of forcefully extracting all the brass and live cartridges from the chambers and dropping them simultaneously out of the cylinder. This technique is used when the shooter wishes to reload the revolver quickly.

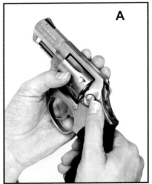
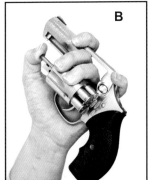
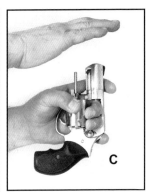

To unload a double-action revolver, grasp the gun in the right hand and disengage the cylinder latch (A). The cylinder is pushed out to the left, in the same manner as when starting the loading procedure. The ejector rod is then pushed fully rearward (B) with the left-hand thumb to extract the spent cartridge cases or live cartridges, which may then be removed manually. Alternatively, the revolver may be pointed upward, and the ejector rod pressed smartly with the right hand (C) to drop the empty cartridge cases and live cartridges out of the chambers.

Unloading Single-Action Revolvers

As with the loading process, the single-action revolver can be unloaded with the revolver held in either hand.

With the revolver held in the right hand, the trigger finger outside of the trigger guard and straight alongside the frame, and the muzzle pointed in a safe direction, the hammer is put in the half-cock position (with some models), and the loading gate opened with the right thumb. The cylinder is

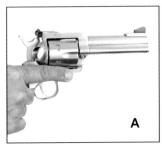
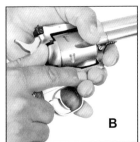
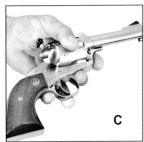

To unload a single-action revolver, the gun is grasped in the firing hand, with the finger outside the trigger guard and the hammer down (A). The loading gate is opened (B), and the cylinder is rotated to align an empty case or live cartridge with the opening gate (C). Note that some revolver designs require that the hammer be in the half-cock mode for the loading gate to be opened and the cylinder rotated.

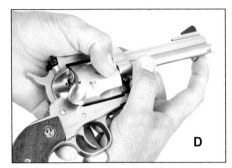

With an empty case or live cartridge aligned with the loading gate, the index finger of the firing hand engages the ejector rod (D) and pulls the rod rearward to push the case or cartridge out of the chamber (E), where it is manually removed. The cylinder is rotated to the next chamber, and the process repeated until the revolver cylinder is empty.

rotated until a cartridge case head is fully visible, and then the ejector, located under the barrel, is pulled to the rear, pushing the live round or empty brass out of the chamber. The ejector is allowed to return forward, the cylinder is rotated to the next chamber, and the process is repeated until all chambers are empty.

For left-handed shooters, the unloading process starts with the revolver in the left hand. With the trigger finger outside of the trigger guard and straight alongside the frame, and the muzzle pointed in a safe direction, the hammer is put in the half-cock position (if necessary), and the loading gate opened with the right hand. The cylinder is rotated until a cartridge case head is fully visible, and then the ejector, located under the barrel, is pulled to the rear, pushing the live cartridge or empty brass out of the chamber. The ejector is allowed to return forward, the cylinder is rotated to the next chamber, and the process is repeated until all chambers are empty.

CHAPTER 7

OPERATING DOUBLE-AND SINGLE-ACTION SEMI-AUTOMATIC PISTOLS

Gun handling consists of the processes to safely and efficiently load, fire, and unload the pistol. As with single- and double-action revolvers, there are specific techniques for performing these functions with single- and double-action semi-automatic pistols.

LOADING

Loading means filling an empty gun with cartridges. This process involves, first, loading the empty magazine and then inserting the magazine into the gun and feeding a live cartridge into the chamber.

Loading the Semi-Automatic Pistol Magazine

The magazine should be grasped by the fingers of the weak (non-firing) hand, with the top of the magazine facing upward and the front of the magazine oriented toward the firing hand. The firing hand picks up a live cartridge and brings it to the top of the magazine, with the case head facing the magazine and the bullet pointing away from the magazine. The case rim is used to depress the magazine follower slightly, and the car-

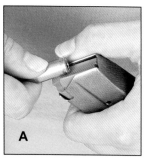 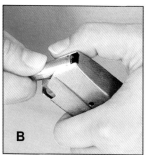 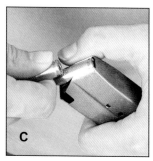

To load a pistol magazine, hold it in the non-firing hand, with its top upward and its front facing the strong hand (A). Grasp a live cartridge in the firing hand, and use the case rim to depress the magazine follower (B). Then slide the cartridge under the feed lips all the way to the rear (C). This process is repeated until the magazine is loaded to full capacity.

tridge is then slid under the feed lips of the magazine all the way to the rear. The case rim of the next cartridge to be loaded depresses the top cartridge in the magazine, and itself is slid under the magazine feed lips. This process is repeated for each cartridge until the magazine is loaded. Finally, the shooter should slap the rear of the loaded magazine sharply, to ensure that all cartridges are positioned to the rear of the unit, for proper feeding.

Loading Semi-Automatic Pistols

The pistol is grasped with the firing hand, with the trigger finger outside the trigger guard, straight along the frame. With the pistol pointing in a safe direction, the non-firing hand brings the magazine to the magazine well in the butt of the gun, and inserts the magazine fully. The magazine must be inserted in the proper orientation, with the bullets facing forward. Normally, a click is heard when the magazine is fully seated. The shooter may also slap the floorplate or basepad to ensure proper seating.

Next, with the pistol still pointed in a safe direction, and the trigger finger still outside the trigger guard, the non-firing hand grasps the slide and

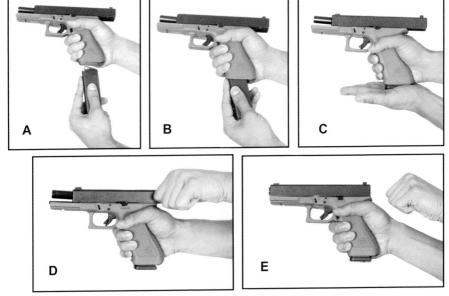

To load a semi-automatic pistol, the pistol is grasped in the firing hand, and the magazine, held in the support hand with the cartridges facing forward, is brought to the pistol's magazine well (A) where it is inserted (B) and fully seated (C). The slide is then fully retracted (D) and released to fly forward and chamber the top cartridge (E).

NRA Guide to the Basics of Pistol Shooting

retracts it. There are different ways of grasping the slide; with any method, the hand must stay well clear of the gun's muzzle.

Retracting the slide allows the top cartridge in the magazine to rise to a position where it can be fed into the chamber when the slide goes forward. There are two ways of accomplishing this. One is to retract the slide fully with the support hand, and then let it fly forward. Alternatively, the slide may be fully retracted with the support hand until it is locked open by the *slide lock*. When loading is desired, the slide lock is depressed, releasing the slide. With either procedure, the forward-moving slide will strip the top cartridge from the magazine and chamber it.

It is critical to avoid following the slide or easing it down with the non-firing hand. Semi-automatic pistols are designed to function best when the slide travels rapidly forward under the pressure of the recoil spring. Easing the slide down is very likely to produce feeding malfunctions.

Once a live cartridge has been chambered, the shooter may commence firing. If there is to be a delay in firing, the pistol should be made safe by either engaging the decocker (on a double-action pistol) or the manual safety (on a single-action pistol), normally positioned near the firing-hand thumb. The location of these controls will be found in the owner's manual for the pistol.

While many modern pistols have ambidextrous controls that are equally convenient for right- and left-handed users, some are designed only for right-handed use. Left-handed shooters using such pistols may have to engage the pistol's decocker or safety with the fingers of their non-firing hand, or develop strong-hand techniques for accomplishing this.

It is also worth noting that some semi-automatic pistols, such as double-action-only models, lack either a decocker or a manual safety.

FIRING

Firing the loaded semi-automatic pistol involves essentially the same procedure whether the gun used is a double-action or single-action type. The pistol is grasped in the firing hand (or in both hands, if a two-hand hold is used). With the pistol pointed in a safe direction and the trigger finger outside the trigger guard, alongside the frame, the gun's decocker or manual safety is moved to the "fire" position, usually by the thumb of the firing hand. With some firearms, however, left-handed shooters will have to operate these controls with the fingers of the non-firing hand.

The pistol is then aligned with the target. At this time, the trigger finger may enter the trigger guard and contact the trigger, and the sequence of events that culminate in firing a shot can begin.

Upon firing the first shot, the shooter may continue to fire a number of shots or may elect to lower the pistol. Alternatively, the shooter may put the loaded pistol on the shooting bench. If the gun is simply lowered, and another shot is to be immediately fired, there is no need to engage the decocker or safety. On the other hand, a loaded pistol placed on a bench should, at the very least, have the decocker or safety put into the "safe" condition. Also, if the pistol is put on the shooting bench and the shooter intends to walk away from it for a moment for any reason, the pistol should be fully unloaded and left on the bench with the slide locked open and the magazine removed.

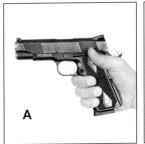 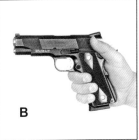 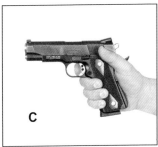

Firing a semi-automatic pistol. With the pistol pointed in a safe direction, and the trigger finger outside the trigger guard (A), the decocker or safety is moved to the "fire" position (B). When the gun is aligned with the target, the trigger finger is placed inside the trigger guard and the trigger is pulled, firing the gun (C).

DECOCKING

Safely lowering the cocked hammer of a semi-automatic pistol with a decocking mechanism usually involves nothing more than activating the decocking lever. With pistols lacking this mechanism, such as single-action semi-automatics, a different procedure must be employed, unload the gun, and refer to the gun's owner's manual.

UNLOADING

To unload a semi-automatic pistol, first ensure that it is pointed in a safe direction. Remove the trigger finger from the trigger and place it outside the trigger guard, alongside the frame. Next, press the magazine release button to drop the magazine from the gun. In most modern pistols, this button is located to the rear of the trigger guard, near the firing-hand thumb. As with other pistol controls, some firearms offer ambidextrous magazine releases that are equally convenient for both right- and left-hand users. Left-handed shooters operating right-handed guns will have to depress the magazine release button either with the tip of the trigger finger, or with the fingers of the non-firing hand. Note that some semi-automatic pistols (mostly older models) do not have a magazine release near the trigger guard, but instead feature a latch at the rear of the magazine well, typically operated by the non-firing hand.

Once the magazine is removed from the pistol, it is still necessary to extract the live cartridge from the chamber. With the pistol kept pointed in a safe direction, and the trigger finger still outside the trigger guard, use the support hand to sharply retract the slide fully to the rear. This will extract the live round from the chamber and eject it. Do not attempt to catch or capture the cartridge flying out of the ejection port. At this time, with the slide fully rearward, visually inspect the chamber to ensure that it is empty.

If further shooting is anticipated, the pistol may be left on the shooting bench with the slide locked open and the magazine removed. On the other hand, if the firearm is to be put back into its case, the slide should be eased forward and, while the gun is pointed in a safe direction, the hammer dropped either by engaging the decocker or by pulling the trigger on the empty chamber. Some semi-automatic pistols, most notably rimfire pistols, can be damaged by dry-firing them. With any pistol, the owner's manual should be consulted to determine if dry-firing is safe to do.

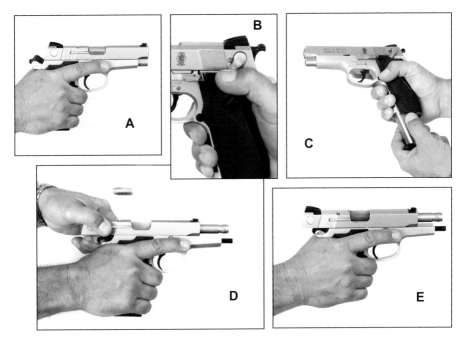

To unload a semi-automatic pistol, first put the trigger finger along the frame, out of the trigger guard (A), engage the safety or decocker if present (B), remove the magazine (C), and retract the slide forcefully to eject any live cartridge that may be in the chamber (D). The slide is then locked back (E) and the chamber visually inspected to ensure it is empty.

CHAPTER 8

AMMUNITION FUNDAMENTALS

While much attention is paid to pistol design and performance, shooters sometimes forget that it is the cartridge that largely determines the performance of any firearm system. Just as a computer is no more than a device for running software, a pistol is only a tool for getting the most out of a particular cartridge.

CARTRIDGE TYPES

There are two types of metallic cartridges used in modern firearms: *rimfire cartridges* and *centerfire cartridges*. These two cartridge types

Cutaway drawings showing rimfire (l.) and centerfire cartridge cases. Priming compound is shown in green.

differ in the location of the pressure-sensitive priming mixture that ignites the gunpowder when the firing pin strikes the case head. In a rimfire cartridge, the priming mixture is contained in a fold in the cartridge rim. In a centerfire cartridge, the priming mixture is contained in a separate component called a *primer*, located in the center of the case head. These differences are explained below.

CARTRIDGE COMPONENTS

There are four parts to any modern cartridge: *case, powder, primer* (or *priming compound*) and *bullet*.

Case components.

Case. Modern cartridge cases are generally made of brass (occasionally of steel); some are nickel-plated. The case consists of a *body*, which terminates at one end in a *neck* and *mouth*, and, at the other, in a thick *head*. A centerfire cartridge case head contains a *primer pocket* that holds the primer, and a *flash hole* that conveys the primer spark through the *web* of the case to the *powder charge*. The head also contains a *headstamp* of the cartridge name. A rimfire case head has no primer, but instead has priming compound located in a fold in the case rim (see **Primer** section, below).

Straight (l.) and bottleneck cases.

There are several types of cases, based on the shapes of the body and head. Case bodies are either of *bottleneck design*, with a neck smaller than the body and a pronounced shoulder where they meet, or *straight*, with a body about the same size as the neck. Case heads come in five configurations. *Rimmed* cases have a protruding rim that is grasped by the pistol's extractor to remove it from the chamber. *Semi-rimmed* cases have a rim that is only slightly larger than the body diameter, and an extractor groove that allows the extractor a better grip. *Rimless cases* have a deep extractor groove that

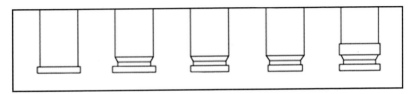

Case head types. From left, rimmed, semi-rimmed, rimless, rebated-rimless, and belted rimless. Most revolver cartridges are of rimmed design, while cartridges for semi-automatic pistols are usually of rimless design.

NRA Guide to the Basics of Pistol Shooting

creates a rim the same diameter as the case body, while *rebated-rimless* cases have a rim smaller in diameter than the body. Finally, *belted rimless* cases are simply rimless cases with a thickened belt directly above the extractor groove. These are used for *magnum* cartridges (cartridges having a larger-than-normal case capacity to develop higher velocity).

Regardless of its design, the case performs the same functions. It contains the other cartridge components; it locates the bullet in relation to the bore and rifling; and it provides a combustion chamber for uniform ballistics. Upon cartridge ignition, it contains the pressure created by propellant gases, and, perhaps most importantly, it expands tightly against the chamber walls, preventing gas leakage to the rear. Finally, after the bullet leaves the muzzle and gas pressure drops, the case springs back slightly from the chamber walls, allowing it to be easily extracted.

Primer. The primer creates the spark that ignites the powder charge. It is essentially a small metal *cup* containing a layer of pressure-sensitive *priming compound*, over which is placed an *anvil* whose pointed tip bears against this compound. When the trigger is pulled, the firing pin sharply hits and indents the primer cup, pushing it against the anvil. This, in turn, compresses the priming compound, igniting it and creating a spark that goes through a *flash hole* to the powder. Such primers are located in the center of the case head; cartridges so configured are thus called *center-fire* cartridges.

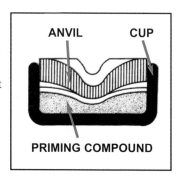

Cutaway of primer components, showing cup, priming compound and anvil.

Some cartridges lack a central primer, but instead have a thin layer of priming compound that coats the bottom of the inside of the case, including the portion of the case that is folded to create a rim. With such cartridges, the firing pin hits the exposed case rim, indenting the thin metal and compressing the priming compound to create a spark. Today's *rimfire* cartridges are limited to relatively low-power .17- and .22-cal. rounds.

Powder. Though all firearms once used black powder to propel the bullet, ammunition for modern arms uses *smokeless powder*, which is made primarily of nitrocellulose (so-called *single-base powders*) or a combination of nitrocellulose and nitroglycerin (*double-base powders*). When the powder is ignited by the primer, it is rapidly converted to a large volume of hot, expanding gas that greatly increases the pressure inside the case, and pushes the bullet down the barrel at high velocity.

Smokeless powder is a propellant that burns at a controlled rate. Thus, powders for different purposes have different compositions, coatings, granule shapes and granule sizes, to produce optimal performance within safe pressure limits.

Bullet. Pistol bullets may have a variety of shapes and types of construction. Most are of lead or jacketed lead construction. In the former, the bullet is cast or swaged to the proper diameter and shape. In the latter type of construction, the bullet has a lead core surrounded by a thin copper

Pistol cartridges may have a variety of bullet shapes and types of construction. From l., lead wadcutter, lead round-nose, lead semi-wadcutter, jacketed soft-nose, semi-jacketed hollow-point, full metal jacket, jacketed truncated cone, jacketed hollow-point.

jacket. Jacketed lead bullets can be driven to higher velocities, and can be designed to give optimum terminal performance for the intended purpose. Additionally, some pistol bullets for hunting or self-defense use are also made out of a solid copper alloy.

Bullet performance in both the air and at the target depends upon bullet construction and shape. More information on pistol bullet performance is contained in Chapter 16: Selecting Pistols, Pistol Ammunition and Accessories.

CARTRIDGE FIRING SEQUENCE

The firing of a cartridge in a firearm follows a specific sequence of events, as shown in the accompanying drawing. Starting with a cartridge in the chamber and the breech closed (A), the trigger is pulled, causing the firing pin to hit the cartridge primer (B) or cartridge rim, in the case of

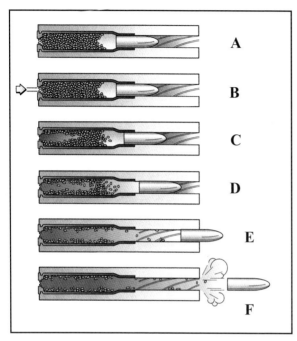

A

B

C

D

E

F

rimfire cartridges. The primer explodes with a hot spark that ignites the gunpowder in the case (C). As the gunpowder burns, it creates high-pressure gas that begins to push the bullet down the bore (D). Increasing pressure in the chamber also causes the case to expand outward tightly against the chamber walls, preventing gas leakage to the rear. Continued combustion of the gunpowder accelerates the bullet completely through the bore (E), until it leaves the muzzle (F). The hot, high-velocity gas exiting the muzzle makes a loud "bang" when it hits the surrounding atmosphere.

CARTRIDGE NOMENCLATURE

Cartridge nomenclature can be confusing, as there has never been a standardized procedure for naming cartridges. Basically, pistol cartridge names have two parts. The first part of the name is a number, either in millimeters or in decimal inch measurements (known as caliber), that represents either the bullet or bore diameter (often only approximately). Sometimes there are two numbers; European cartridges in particular are designated by both the bullet diameter in millimeters and the case length in millimeters (e.g., 9 X 19 mm).

The second part of the designation is far more variable, and may represent any of several things: the name of the company responsible for the cartridge's development (.40 Smith & Wesson); the individual (.454 Casull) who originated or designed the cartridge; a popular or descriptive name (.38 Special); or, with military-designed cartridges, the firearm in

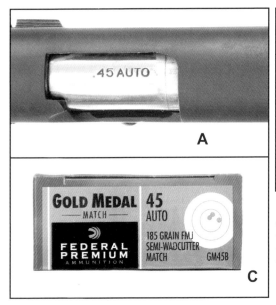

The proper ammunition for a given pistol is determined by matching the markings on the barrel (A) with the cartridge designation on the headstamp (B) and the cartridge box (C).

which it was used (.455 Webley). A few cartridges have both decimal and metric designations, such as the .32 ACP and 7.65 mm Auto. Finally, some cartridges may be known by more than one name (9 mm Para, 9 mm Parabellum, 9 mm Luger, 9X19 mm).

For the pistol owner to select the proper ammunition for his or her firearm, all that is required is to match the designation on the barrel and/or slide with that on the cartridge box and the cartridge headstamp. If the barrel or slide of the firearm lacks a cartridge designation, or if there is a suspicion that the pistol may have been modified to fire a cartridge other than what is indicated by the markings, the gun should be taken to a competent gunsmith (usually listed in the Yellow Pages) for an evaluation.

AMMUNITION SAFETY

The primary factor in ammunition safety involves using the proper ammunition for the firearm. As mentioned above, the pistol shooter must ensure that the designation on the cartridge box, headstamp and gun barrel or slide all match.

Cartridges designated +P and +P+ are loaded to higher pressures than standard cartridges, and must only be used in guns certified for them.

Check the markings on the gun, the pistol's owner's manual, or contact the manufacturer to verify that your gun can safely fire +P or +P+ cartridges. It should also be noted that some pistols are chambered for low-pressure cartridges that are identical in dimensions to higher-pressure rounds (such as the .38 Auto and .38 Super Auto +P). Such higher-pressure cartridges should never be fired in a gun designed for lower-pressure ammunition.

Ammunition in Fires. Extensive tests have shown that ammunition in a fire does not explode, or propel the bullet to dangerous velocities. In general, cartridges exposed to fire will burst, propelling the bullet only a few feet. The primer may be expelled at relatively high velocity, as well as small shards of brass from the ruptured case, but these objects generally represent a danger only to the eyes, and only at very close range.

Safe Ammunition Storage. Ammunition should be stored in a cool and dry place; it can withstand the normal variations in temperature and humidity found in the typical home environment. Prolonged exposure to high temperatures is to be avoided. Also to be avoided is contamination by water, solvents, lubricants and so forth. Store ammunition in a location off the floor and protected from exposure to water, as from a leaky roof or damp basement.

Ammunition should also be stored in a manner to keep it from unauthorized persons, such as children and visitors to the home. Each gun owner has to determine what level of security is best suited for his or her environment. In some cases, the pistol owner may choose to keep ammunition in a lockable container. Most gun shops will be able to make recommendations regarding the type of lockable container suitable for this purpose.

Disposal of Unserviceable Ammunition. Ammunition that has been in a flood or fire, has been immersed in water, or has been exposed to solvents, oils or other liquids, should not be fired. Instead, such ammunition should be considered unserviceable and must be disposed of. Never dispose of such ammunition by burying, dumping in a waterway, or selling it at a yard sale. Proper disposal methods include delivery to a hazardous materials disposal center; or return of the unserviceable ammunition to the original manufacturer.

More information on ammunition safety can be found in free brochures from the Sporting Arms and Ammunition Manufacturers' Institute (SAAMI), 11 Mile Hill Road, Newtown, CT 06470-2359.

Cartridge malfunctions. There are three types of cartridge malfunctions: misfire, hangfire, and squib load.

A *misfire* is the failure of a cartridge to ignite when the primer or case rim has been struck by the firing pin. This situation may be caused by a defect in the cartridge or by a defect in the pistol that causes a weak firing pin strike.

A *hangfire* is a perceptible delay in the ignition of a cartridge after the primer or case rim has been struck by the firing pin. This delay may last several seconds. When a cartridge fails to fire immediately, it will not be known at first if the problem is a misfire or a hangfire. Therefore, keep the pistol pointed in a safe direction, as a hangfire condition might exist and cause the pistol to fire after a substantial delay. Don't attempt to open the action of the pistol to remove the cartridge for at least 30 seconds.

A *squib load* occurs when the cartridge develops less than normal pressure or velocity after ignition of a cartridge. Squib loads can cause a bullet to fail to exit the muzzle and become lodged in the bore. If anything unusual is noticed upon firing a shot, such as a reduction in noise, muzzle flash, or recoil, a squib load should be suspected. Stop firing immediately and, keeping the muzzle pointed in a safe direction, unload the pistol and check to ensure that all chambers are empty. Then, with the action open, carefully run a cleaning rod through the barrel to be sure that it is not obstructed. If a bullet is lodged in the barrel, the firing of another shot could cause injury or damage to the gun.

PART III

BUILDING PISTOL SHOOTING SKILLS

CHAPTER 9

FUNDAMENTALS OF PISTOL SHOOTING

Successful pistol shooting is based upon the fundamental principles of marksmanship. These fundamentals are *aiming, breath control, hold control, trigger control* and *follow-through*. Although these fundamentals may be applied in different ways, depending upon whether the pistol is used for plinking, hunting, formal target shooting or self-defense, they must always be observed for the most consistent results.

Prior to mastering these fundamentals, the pistol shooter must address two other critical aspects of technique: *hand and eye dominance*, and *grip*.

HAND AND EYE DOMINANCE

Shooting any firearm involves coordination between the eyes and hands. For the majority of people, best shooting is accomplished by firing the gun with the dominant hand and aiming with the dominant eye.

Most people have a *dominant hand*, making them definitely right- or left-handed. Relatively few people are truly *ambidextrous*, or able to perform skills involving manual dexterity equally well with either hand. In

Establishing eye dominance. First, focus on a distant object with both eyes open (A). Extend the arms forward with the hands brought together to form a hole between the thumbs, and look at the object through this hole (B). Bring the hands close to the face, still observing the object (C). When the hands are just a few inches from the face, the hole between the hands will be directly in front of the dominant eye.

most cases, the dominant hand is easily determined, as it is the hand that is used for most one-handed tasks. The dominant hand and arm are often stronger and demonstrate better coordination.

Just as one hand tends to be dominant over the other, the brain also has a preference for one eye over the other, which is known as *eye dominance*. Most often the dominant eye is on the same side as the dominant hand, but there are many individuals in whom this is not the case. Many people are not even aware that they have a dominant eye, as in almost all normal activities, both eyes act in concert, and there are few if any normal activities in which one eye only is used. Eye dominance is important in shooting, however, as only one eye is used to aim.

Determining eye dominance is easily accomplished through the following exercise. With both eyes open, focus on a small object at some distance (at least 10-12 feet away). Then extend both hands forward at arm's length, bring the hands together to form a small hole between the webs of the thumbs, and look at the distant object through this hole. Slowly bring the hands to the face, keeping the object in view through the hole between the hands. When the hands are only a few inches from the face, they will be in front of one eye or the other. That eye is the dominant eye. Alternatively, this exercise may be done using a shooting partner, coach or firearm instructor to observe which eye is dominant.

GRIP

There are many shooting positions which may be used for firing a pistol, some of which are specific to certain shooting disciplines. Even before any shooting positions can be introduced, the new pistol shooter must know how to assume a proper one- or two-handed grip.

The Two-Handed Grip

For most pistol shooting activities, a two-handed grip will be used. The vast majority of pistol shooters find that such a grip provides more control of the firearm, steadier aiming, better recoil absorption, and stronger gun retention.

To assume the grip, first grasp the pistol behind the muzzle in the support (non-firing) hand. Make a "Y" of the thumb and fingers of the firing hand (A), and place the gun's backstrap firmly in the web of the firing-hand thumb (B). When this is done, wrap the firing-hand fingers around the pistol's grip (C).

Next, bring the support hand around the front of the grip (D) so that its fingers overlie and overlap the firing-hand fingers (E). The knuckles of the

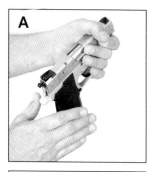

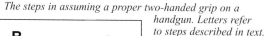

The steps in assuming a proper two-handed grip on a handgun. Letters refer to steps described in text.

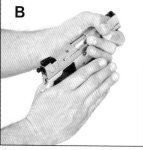

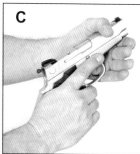

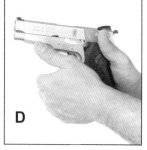

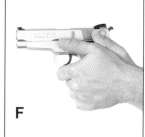

second joint of the support-hand fingers should be roughly aligned with the same knuckles of the firing hand. Gripping the gun with tension from both the support and firing hands creates a steadier hold on the pistol.

With a semi-automatic pistol, the support-hand thumb should lie directly forward of and below the shooting-hand thumb (F). With a revolver, the support-hand thumb lies directly overtop the firing-hand thumb (G).

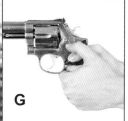

Grip consistency is essential for accurate shooting. Use dry-fire practice to check and reinforce the correct trigger finger placement. Note that the proper grip for one firearm may not be appropriate for another firearm; your grip may vary depending upon the shape of a gun's grip frame. Also, your grip may vary slightly from position to position.

The One-Handed Grip

The one-handed grip was at one time the most common way to hold a pistol. Today it is used primarily in certain forms of target competition, such as NRA and International bullseye shooting. One-handed shooting may also be practiced by those who own a pistol for self-defense. A description of the one-handed grip is found in Appendix A: The One-Handed Shooting Position.

AIMING

Aiming is the process of aligning a firearm with a target so that a bullet fired from that firearm will strike the target where desired. In other words, the point of aim will coincide with the point of impact. Aiming is accomplished using the gun's sights. Most pistols feature *iron sights* (non-optical sights) consisting of a flat-topped front post and a square-cornered rear notch.

Aiming consists of two stages: *sight alignment* and *sight picture*. *Sight alignment* refers to the proper positioning of the shooting eye, the rear sight, and the front sight in relation to each other. With the notch-and-post system on most pistols, proper sight alignment for precise shooting occurs when the front post is centered laterally in the rear notch, with the same amount of space on either side of the post, and the tops of both the post and the notch are aligned.

Aiming involves both the proper relationship between the front and rear sights (sight alignment) and the proper relationship of the aligned sights with the target (sight picture).

Sight picture refers to the relationship between the gun's properly aligned sights and the target. This relationship will vary, depending upon the pistol shooting activity in which one is engaged. In traditional bullseye target shooting, the aligned sights are placed at the 6 o'clock position in relation to the round black bull. In other target sports, such as pistol silhouette, cowboy action and practical pistol shooting, the aligned sights are placed at the center of the target. In hunting, the proper sight picture depends upon the vital area of the game being hunted. And for defensive shooting purposes, the pistol's aligned sights are placed on the center of exposed mass of the target. That is, the sights are placed in the middle of the target area that is exposed. Note that the 6 o'clock hold used with bullseye targets applies only to iron sights. Shooters using optical (telescopic) sights or red-dot sights put the crosshairs or dot exactly at the spot on the target where a hit is desired.

Visual focus with iron pistol sights should be on the front sight. This will often make both the rear sight and the target somewhat blurry, but in almost all situations they will be sufficiently clear for the shooter to establish good sight alignment and proper sight picture.

BREATH CONTROL

Breath control is the method used to minimize gun movement due to breathing. With each breath, your ribcage expands and your shoulders rise slightly. This movement is transmitted to your arms, causing your pistol to shift position in relation to the target.

In pistol activities involving a deliberate and unhurried pace of shooting, breath control is achieved by simply taking a few normal breaths, expelling about half the air out of the lungs, and then holding the breath for the few seconds required to fire the shot. Typically, maximum steadiness is achieved within about three to eight seconds after breathing has stopped; the shot should thus be fired within that time period. After the shot is fired, the shooter relaxes, resumes breathing and starts the process over again.

In any situation in which the shooter may need to fire a shot quickly, under mental or physical stress, the heart will be pounding and the lungs will be demanding air. Breath control under these circumstances involves simply stopping breathing and holding it. Breathing should simply cease momentarily while the shot is being fired. This will steady the position and allow for a quick shot or series of shots.

HOLD CONTROL

Maximum accuracy is achieved when the firearm is held motionless during the process of aiming and firing. *Hold control* is the method by which both the body and the gun are held as still as possible during the period of time when the shot is fired.

Hold control is achieved primarily through a proper grip, and a well-balanced, stable shooting position that is naturally aligned with the target, as well as extensive practice. Physical fitness and good muscle tone also contribute to a steady hold. Some positions allow a more stable hold than others. More information on positions and on target alignment is found in Chapter 10: Fundamentals of Pistol Shooting Positions.

Some novice shooters make the mistake of firing a string of shots without allowing the arm and shoulder muscles to rest. The first two or three shots may be fired accurately, but by the fifth or sixth shot, muscle fatigue sets in, producing tremors and other movement that prevent good shooting.

Until the muscles that hold and support the pistol are strengthened, the shooter should fire only a few shots, and then lower the gun to rest.

TRIGGER CONTROL

Trigger control is one of the most important shooting fundamentals. The term refers to the technique of pulling the trigger without causing any movement of the aligned sights.

Proper trigger control is achieved by applying gradually increasing pressure to the trigger until the shot is fired. This pressure is applied in a rearward direction, not to the side or up or down. The goal of this technique is to produce a "surprise break," in which the shooter cannot predict the exact moment at which the gun will fire.

A surprise break is desired to prevent the shooter from anticipating the shot. New shooters are not accustomed to the recoil, flash and blast that occur when a gun is fired, and thus are prone to reacting more or less instinctively by tightening their muscles, squinting their eyes, and making movements that attempt to counteract the gun's recoil. These involuntary movements are collectively called *flinching* or a*nticipating the shot,* and have a negative effect on accuracy by disturbing sight alignment and sight picture just before the shot is fired.

Even in a shooting situation in which a slow, gradual pull may not be possible, such as during a hunt or a defensive encounter, trigger control should still be practiced. In such situations, trigger control involves speeding up the process of squeezing the trigger without jerking or flinching. The smoother the trigger is pulled, the less the gun's sights will be disturbed during the firing process, even when the time period is compressed.

Good trigger control also involves the proper placement of the trigger finger on the trigger. A properly placed trigger finger allows the force of the pull to be directed straight to the rear, minimizing a tendency to jerk the gun to the right or left. Proper placement also allows the gun to be

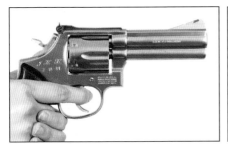

Proper trigger finger placement on a revolver.

Proper shooting trigger finger placement on a semi-automatic pistol.

fired by moving only the trigger finger.

For single-action shooting, the trigger should be pulled using the middle of the last pad of the trigger finger. For double-action shooting, the trigger should be placed approximately on the joint between the last and middle pads of the trigger finger. The ideal trigger finger placement can be achieved through dry-fire practice at a sheet of white paper. Adjust your finger position until there is no movement in sight alignment when the trigger is pulled and the hammer or striker falls. Note that the proper contact point on the trigger finger may change from gun to gun and firing position to firing position.

If possible, there should also be a small gap between the trigger finger

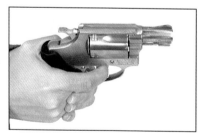
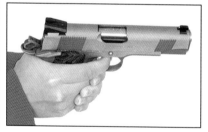

The proper gap between the trigger finger and the frame of a revolver (left) and a semi-automatic pistol.

and the pistol frame to prevent the finger from contacting or dragging on the frame and thus disturbing sight alignment as the trigger is pulled.

FOLLOW-THROUGH

The concept of *follow-through* is common to many sports, such as golf, tennis, baseball, bowling and archery. In shooting, follow-through is the effort made by the shooter to integrate, maintain and continue all shooting fundamentals before, during and immediately after firing the shot. It is true that any alteration in the gun position, stance, sight alignment, and so forth that occurs after the bullet has left the muzzle has no effect whatsoever on accuracy or shot placement. Nonetheless, it is important to consciously maintain the shooting fundamentals for a brief time after the shot has been fired because only by doing so will you be absolutely certain that those fundamentals are applied before and during the firing of the shot. Thus, proper follow-through minimizes gun movement as the shot is

fired. A shooter who fails to follow through and applies the fundamentals only up to the breaking of the trigger will (in anticipation of the shot) sooner or later abandon one or more of the fundamentals just prior to firing, resulting in errant bullet flight and poor grouping.

Proper follow-through does more than just ensure adherence to the shooting fundamentals through the firing of the shot. Follow-through also

Proper follow-through, as well as good recoil control, combine to allow this shooter to fire several accurate shots in rapid succession.

sets up any successive shots, whenever a shooter may be called upon to fire multiple times accurately and rapidly. The follow-through used in these situations is highly compressed to last only a fraction of a second, but still allows the shooter to maintain a position in alignment with the target and to quickly recover the proper sight picture.

During follow-through, the trigger finger pressure is relaxed, allowing the trigger to reset. However, the trigger finger still maintains contact with the trigger face.

All of the fundamentals of pistol shooting are integrated in the firing of a shot, no matter what the target. The shooter aims (maintaining both sight alignment and the proper sight picture) while momentarily stopping respiration (breath control) and movement (hold control). Only the trigger finger, properly placed, is moved to fire the shot (trigger control). Before, during and after the shot is fired, the shooter observes all the proper shooting fundamentals (follow-through). The two most important fundamentals are aiming and trigger control.

CHAPTER 10

FUNDAMENTALS OF PISTOL SHOOTING POSITIONS

As presented in the previous chapter, the fundamentals of pistol marksmanship are observed regardless of the type of pistol shooting being performed. Effective shooting takes more than just adherence to these fundamentals, however. An effective *shooting position* is the platform from which the fundamentals are applied.

ELEMENTS OF A SHOOTING POSITION

Although there are many effective shooting positions for different situations, all share a number of common characteristics: *consistency, balance, support, natural aiming area* and *comfort*.

Consistency

Consistency is critical because variations in position produce variations in impact point and/or group size. You must strive to assume each position in the same exact way every time.

In the training phase, this is accomplished by conscious attention to each aspect of the position and each step taken to assume it. With repetition, this process of developing a position "by the numbers" will become ingrained in your subconscious, eventually enabling you to flow into the position quickly, effortlessly, naturally and consistently. The "muscle memory" thus developed through rigorous practice will allow the position to be assumed easily and automatically.

A balanced shooting position.

Balance

Balance is also an essential component of a proper firing position. Balance is usually best achieved in a stance with the feet spaced at shoulders-width, even weight distribution, and a slightly forward lean with the majority of the weight on the balls of the feet.

A balanced position provides the most stable shooting platform, one that absorbs recoil and facilitates both movement and accurate follow-up shots. A balanced position with the head upright and level also is important for controlling body movement. The brain senses body position by a number of mechanisms, including a structure in the inner ear known as the labyrinth. An upright, level head position will maximize the ability of the labyrinth to promote body equilibrium and efficient body movement.

Support

A good position also offers *support* to minimize gun movement while aiming. Support can be provided by the skeleton, muscle tension or an external object, such as sandbags on a bench. A two-handed grip, for example, efficiently uses muscle tension to provide more support than a one-handed grip. Generally, standing positions offer less support than kneeling and prone positions. The benchrest position provides the most support of any shooting position. Even the more limited support offered by one-handed positions can be maximized by ensuring that the stance is balanced, the grip is firm, and the shooter is properly aligned with the target.

The benchrest position, in which sandbags are used to support the wrists, offers the greatest shooting support.

Natural Aiming Area (NAA)

All effective firing positions incorporate the shooter's natural aiming area (NAA). NAA refers to the natural alignment of the shooter and the gun in

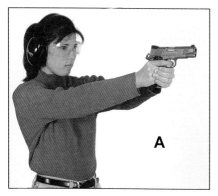

In the NAA (Natural Aiming Area) exercise, the shooter first assumes a position with the gun aimed at a target (A). Then the eyes are closed, and the gun moved in a small circle (B) until it comes to rest in the position that feels most naturally stable and comfortable. The eyes are then opened (C) and the shooter observes where the pistol's sights are in relation to the target. If the "wobble area" of the sights is not centered on the target, the shooter's foot position or some other aspect of the stance should be modified to achieve the proper sight picture while taking advantage of her body's natural alignment.

A

B

C

any position. To determine your NAA, first assume your position, with your eyes open and your gun aimed at a target. Next, close your eyes. With your eyes still closed, make a circle with the pistol, and then settle into the position that feels most stable and comfortable, and take several breaths. Then, open your eyes and observe where your gun's sights are pointed in relation to the target. Ideally, the sight picture will be aligned with the target. If the sight picture is aligned to the right or left or slightly high or low, you will have to modify your foot position or some other aspect of your stance to achieve the proper natural alignment.

Of course, the sight picture does not stay perfectly still, as it is impossible to hold a pistol without some movement. When proper NAA is achieved, the "wobble area" of the sights will be centered on the target.

Repeat the NAA exercise until your stance is adjusted for the proper natural alignment. You should make every effort to adopt this same alignment each time the stance is assumed in order to take advantage of your NAA. Also, periodically repeat the NAA exercise, as changes in shooting experience, posture, age and so forth can affect the body's natural alignment.

Comfort

Finally, a proper position should be *comfortable*. A stance that is not comfortable—one that is forced, awkward, strained or painful—is unlikely to be consistent or stable, and thus will not contribute to effective shooting. When practicing shooting positions, you should be conscious of how natural and comfortable each position is. Positions that do not feel comfortable must be modified as necessary. However, in some cases discomfort may be the result of the lack of joint flexibility or muscular strength. In such cases, a minimal amount of physical training is usually all that is needed to allow the shooter to comfortably assume a proper shooting position. Of course, any shooter should consult his or her doctor prior to starting any physical training regimen.

LEARNING A SHOOTING POSITION

The pistol shooter may have the need to learn only one or two, or many, shooting positions. Whether the position is simple or complex, the process for mastering it is the same, and involves a specific process.

The first step in learning a shooting position is to *study the position*. This means knowing what is involved in the position, how it is assumed, and the purpose of the position.

The second step is to *practice the position without a pistol*. Just about every shooting position places special demands upon the shooter in terms of balance, coordination, hand and foot placement, and more. Practicing these aspects of the position without a pistol simplifies the position, breaking the learning process into a number of steps that build upon each other.

Next, *practice the position with an unloaded pistol*. Any shooting position can effectively be practiced using an empty gun in the dry-fire mode, with care taken to observe all dry-firing safety rules (see Chapter 17: Pistol Shooting Activities and Opportunities for Skill Development).

During dry-fire practice, *align the position with the target*. Each shooter will have a different alignment with the target for each shooting position. Perform the Natural Aiming Area (NAA) exercise described earlier in this chapter with every shooting position learned.

Once the position has been acquired using an empty gun, *test the position* with live ammunition. Live-fire testing will reveal if there are aspects of the position, or the shooting fundamentals, that need to be corrected.

After the skills presented in this chapter have been mastered, proceed to learning the various shooting positions. The positions taught in the NRA

Basic Pistol Shooting Course are the Benchrest position and the Isosceles two-handed standing position. The Weaver two-handed standing position is also presented in this book. These positions, presented in succeeding chapters, should suffice for the great majority of shooting activities in which the novice will take part. However, because there are some activities, such as NRA bullseye pistol shooting, in which the pistol is fired with one hand only, a single one-handed position is described in Appendix A: The One-Handed Shooting Position.

CHAPTER 11

THE BENCHREST POSITION

The most fundamental position that any new pistol shooter should learn is the benchrest position. The position derives its name from the fact that the shooter fires from a seated position, using a rest on a shooting bench for pistol support.

PREPARING TO USE THE BENCHREST POSITION

Before assuming the benchrest position, a number of items must be assembled. First and foremost is a *shooting bench* approximately 30"-36" high, with sufficient space for the shooter's elbows, sandbag rests, ammunition and spotting scope, if used. Sturdiness and stability are a must; card tables, planks across sawhorses, etc. do not afford the steady rest necessary for accurate shooting. Best are benches designed expressly for shooters; some may have a cutout for the shooter's upper body.

The next requirement is a *chair* or *stool* for use with the shooting bench. This should be high enough so that about half of the shooter's torso is above the bench. Proper height in relation to the shooter's legs is also important. The seat should allow the shooter's feet to be flat on the ground, with an angle at the knee joint of approximately 80-90 degrees. The exact angle will vary

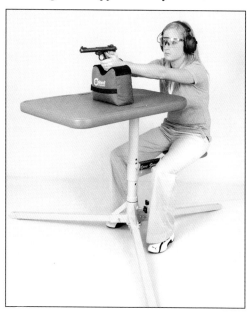

Proper benchrest technique: head erect, back straight, feet solidly on the ground, arms extended, pistol in a proper two-handed grip at eye level, and wrists supported by the sandbag rest.

somewhat, depending upon the leg length of the shooter.

Also needed is a *rest* for supporting the pistol. There are many types of these, from simple sandbags to elaborate devices providing support for both the pistol and the shooting hand, and offering various types of adjustments. Even homemade rests, such as old telephone books or a rolled-up jacket, can be used with some success, although such expedients often do

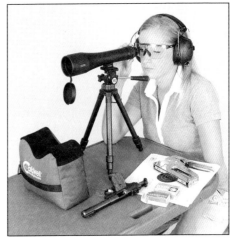

Some of the accessories useful for benchrest shooting: rest, sandbags, spotting scope, targets, pasters, stapler, and eye and hearing protection.

Different types of pistol rests.

not offer the consistent performance of products made specifically for supporting firearms.

Hard-kicking pistols tend to lift the shooting hand and, as a consequence, drive the elbow of the shooting arm downward. Thus, for extended benchrest sessions with heavy-recoiling centerfire pistols, an *elbow pad* is often recommended.

Another accessory that can make the benchrest range session more productive is a spotting scope, an optical device that allows the shooter to see bullet holes at 25 to 50 yards and more. The shooter should also have a supply of targets, a stapler for affixing the targets to a target board or backer, target pasters, and of course, eye and hearing protection. More information on useful shooting accessories is found in Chapter 16: Selecting Pistols, Pistol Ammunition and Accessories.

ASSUMING THE BENCHREST POSITION

Before assuming the benchrest position, assure that the bench and shooting stool are situated on level ground, and do not rock or wobble. Sit at the bench with the chair or stool positioned so as to allow a comfortable, upright position with your feet flat on the ground and your body weight equally distributed. Your upper body should be near the benchtop, but not touching it.

Once a comfortable and stable seated position is achieved, use the unloaded pistol to try different rest positions to find the one offering the greatest stability, balance, and comfort. Rest height is of considerable importance. The proper height allows your arms and elbows to contact the rest and benchtop comfortably and naturally, and allows your head to be in a natural upright position.

There are many ways in which a rest may be used with a pistol. For example, a sandbag may support the wrists and palms, but not the pistol itself. Alternatively, the rest may support some or most of the gun's weight, either on the frame or barrel (if the latter is long enough). With either method, the barrel must protrude significantly—at least 2"—beyond the rest. Also, for best accuracy, the bottom of the gun butt should not contact the bench top or any other hard surface. Finally, it must be remembered that the barrel/cylinder gap of revolvers allows the escape of hot, high-pressure gases, which can discolor any object near this gap.

Once you have obtained a comfortable, stable and balanced position, with the pistol properly supported, dry-fire the pistol to verify the position. A proper position allows the pistol to be held and dry-fired with no movement of the sights.

While the pistol may be fired with one hand, best accuracy, control and hold stability are achieved with a two-handed grip, as presented in Chapter

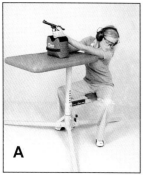 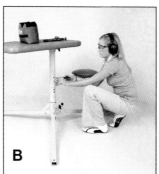 

Proper seat height is critical to the benchrest position. Seat position in (A) is too low; after adjustment (B), seat is at proper height (C).

9: Fundamentals of Pistol Shooting Positions. This is particularly true for heavy-recoiling pistols.

After successfully dry-firing, you may proceed to live ammunition. Recoil may require minor modifications of the position. In general, the most accurate benchrest shooting is done with relaxed hands and arms, rather than a "death grip."

USING THE BENCHREST POSITION TO ZERO THE PISTOL

One of the first tasks any new gun owner must do is to zero the firearm. *Zeroing* involves making the pistol's sights and point of impact coincide, with a particular brand of ammunition at a given distance. The benchrest position is ideal for pistol zeroing because it is the position that affords the least pistol motion and thus greatest accuracy, allowing higher confidence in the observed changes in bullet impact that occur with sight adjustments.

Zeroing an adjustable-sight pistol, or one having a red-dot or telescopic sight, is relatively easy. Use a fairly large target—an 8 1/2" by 11" sheet of paper or larger—with a relatively small aiming point, such as a 1"-diameter dot, in the center. With the target placed in a safe direction about 5-7 yards downrange, fire one to three shots at the dot, concentrating on the shooting fundamentals.

All shots fired should impact close together, forming a *shot group*. If the shots do not coincide with the dot used as an aiming point, the sights must be adjusted. Most commonly, both windage and elevation are adjusted using knobs or screws on the rear sight unit. The rear sight is moved in the

Adjusting iron sights (l.) and a telescopic pistol sight.

direction of the desired change in bullet impact. Thus, if the bullet hits below the aiming point, the rear sight must be adjusted so that the blade sits higher, to raise the location of bullet impact. Similarly, to move bullet impact to the right, the rear sight blade must be moved to the right. Most adjustable rear sights have an engraved arrow or letter to indicate the direction of adjustment achieved by turning the windage and elevation adjusting screws or knobs in a particular direction.

Once the point of aim and the bullet impacts coincide at 7 yards, the target may be moved back to 15 or 25 yards, or further if desired, and the gun re-zeroed for that range. The actual distance for which a gun may be zeroed will vary with the gun's purpose—7-15 yards for most self-defense pistols, and 50-75 yards or more for hunting pistols. For target shooters, the pistol should be zeroed for the precise range(s) used in competition.

Many target-style adjustable sights have "click adjustments" that give the shooter a palpable click each time the adjusting knob or screw is turned through a small arc. Each click produces a standard or predictable amount of change in bullet impact at a known distance (e.g., 1/2" at 50 yards), making precise and repeatable sight adjustments easier.

Red-dot and telescopic sights have similar windage and elevation adjustments, usually by means of knobs or dials that are often located roughly in the middle of the sight. The direction of adjustment, and the value of each click, are normally found on the scope's adjustment knobs or dials. Many click values are given in *minutes of angle* (1 m.o.a.=1.04" at 100 yards). Common click values for pistol scopes are 1/2" and 1/4" at 100 yards, or 1/2 and 1/4 m.o.a. Adjustment instructions and other information are found in each pistol scope's owner's manuals.

Once the gun is zeroed at the desired range with the ammunition to be used, different zeros can be established at different distances, or using different ammunition.

Zeroing pistols with fixed iron sights can be challenging, as there is no easy or precise means to bring the point of aim into alignment with the point of bullet impact. Some changes in elevation can be produced by using different loads. In general, at relatively short distances (25 yards and under), heavier, slower-moving bullets will print higher on a target than lighter, faster-moving bullets. This is because gun recoil begins while the bullet is still in the barrel, and slower-moving bullets are in the

With a given cartridge, it may be necessary to try both high- and low-velocity loads to bring bullet impact into alignment with the point of aim at a specific distance.

barrel longer, and thus exit the bore when the muzzle is elevated at a higher angle due to recoil. Experimentation with different loads will often bring bullet impact acceptably close to the sights' point of aim at a reasonable target distance. When it does not, the only recourse may be for a gunsmith to install a higher front sight (if bullet impact is too high) or remove material from the front sight (if bullet impact is too low).

When the rear fixed sight is mounted on the gun's slide or frame by way of a transverse dovetail, windage adjustments can sometimes be effected simply by drifting the sight laterally in the dovetail. This task is usually best left to a competent pistolsmith.

USING THE BENCHREST POSITION TO IMPROVE PISTOL SHOOTING

Many novice pistol owners, when shooting offhand or from various other pistol positions, spend most of their concentration and energy in trying to hold the pistol steady on target, and, as a result, often fail to observe all the shooting fundamentals. The benchrest position, because it eliminates the need to hold the pistol steady, allows the shooter to focus on the fundamentals, and is thus a good tool for refining shooting technique.

Shooting from the benchrest position is not just for beginners, however. Most top competitive shooters regularly spend time shooting groups from the benchrest position. This activity allows them to consciously focus on, and review, individual aspects of technique.

In addition to technique, many other things may influence shooting accuracy. Accuracy refers to the ability to deliver shots to the point of aim consistently, repeatably and with a high level of precision. Different ammunition loads, gun components such as barrels and triggers, and even accessories such as shooting glasses can all affect the level of accuracy that is achieved. The benchrest position, because it affords the most stable and precise technique for pistol shooting, is ideal for evaluating the effects of different loads, gun modifications and other factors on accuracy. For the same reason, it is the position most often used to perform accuracy comparisons between different guns.

Meaningful accuracy comparisons can only be obtained by the proper testing procedure, performed in a consistent way. For more information on such a procedure, see Chapter 16: Selecting Pistols, Pistol Ammunition and Accessories.

CHAPTER 12

STANDING PISTOL SHOOTING POSITIONS

Except for certain types of pistol competition in which a one-handed position is mandated, most shooters will use two hands to shoot a pistol. A two-hand hold is steadier, allowing greater accuracy, and also permits a faster recovery from recoil, which can be important in hunting, practical pistol competition, or self-defense.

Two basic two-handed shooting positions are presented in this book: the *isosceles position* and the *Weaver position*.

THE ISOSCELES POSITION

The Isosceles position is so named because in this position the extended arms, when seen from above, resemble an isosceles triangle. In the isosceles position, the feet are placed at about shoulders width, and the feet and shoulders are square with the target. The knees are slightly bent and the weight is slightly forward, on the balls of the feet. The pistol is grasped in a normal two-handed grip, and is held with both arms extended fully forward. The elbows are straight but not locked. The head is erect, not hunched; the shoulders are at their normal height, not raised; and the firearm is lifted to the level of the eyes for aiming.

The isosceles position is a very natural shooting position, and may be assumed simply by standing up from the benchrest position, described in Chapter 11: The Benchrest Position. Under stress, many shooters

The isosceles position. The weight is equally distributed on both feet, which are on a line perpendicular to the target. The body is straight or leaning slightly forward, the head is erect, and the pistol is held at eye level in a two-handed hold, with both arms extended fully forward.

The isosceles position, from the front (l.) and from above. Both arms are extended fully forward, approximating an iscosceles triangle when seen from above. The isosceles position is more naturally and easily assumed by many novices.

automatically and reflexively adopt a modified "instinctive" form of the isosceles position.

Should the need arise to address a target at an angle to the original position, a shooter using the isosceles position can simply pivot at the waist. The upper body acts like a turret, easily rotating to the right or left.

The primary advantage of the isosceles position for novice pistol shooters is that it is natural and easy to assume. As mentioned earlier, for most shooters, simply standing up from the benchrest position puts them in a close approximation of the isosceles position.

THE WEAVER
POSITION

The Weaver position is named for former Los Angeles County Sheriff's Deputy Jack Weaver, who is credited with originating it in the late 1950s. To assume the Weaver position, the body should be placed in a rough boxer's stance with the foot on the firing-hand side placed rearward, the support-hand shoulder angled toward the target, the knees slightly flexed and the body weight carried slightly forward, on the balls of the feet. The pistol should be grasped in a normal two-handed grip, but with both elbows bent (the support-hand elbow pointing somewhat downward) to bring the pistol closer to the body than in the isosceles position. The location of the pistol often requires that the head tip slightly to properly view the sights.

Tension between the two hands is perhaps the most functionally significant feature of this position: the firing hand is pushed forward into the support hand, which simultaneously pulls rearward. This push-pull tension creates great stability and steadiness.

The Weaver position gives considerable support to the firearm. Moreover, the Weaver's bent elbows and asymmetrical foot position enhance recoil absorption. When a shot is fired, the bent elbows act as springs, bending to absorb recoil forces and then returning the gun to its original position. With heavy-recoiling pistols, the Weaver position affords fast shot-to-shot recovery for many shooters. Finally, the boxer's stance gives excellent balance and mobility.

The Weaver position's asymmetry puts a greater premium on proper body alignment, however; thus, establishing and maintaining a proper Natural Aiming Area (NAA) with the position is critical. Shooters using the Weaver position should regularly verify their NAA, and adjust the position accordingly. Because of differences in flexibility and body proportions, the exact placement of the feet and the degree of offset of the shoulders will differ for each shooter, and should be established using the NAA exercise as well as actual shooting practice. Some shooters will end up with a Weaver position in which the upper body is only slightly bladed away, and the head held fully upright, while others will turn the upper body away from the target to a greater degree, often requiring a head position that slightly angles or leans toward the shooting-hand side.

Also, different shooters may assume different degrees of flexion at the elbows. For some shooters, the elbow of the shooting hand arm will point nearly straight down at the ground, while the elbow of the support-hand arm will point slightly out to the side. This position places the gun closer to the body, and may be preferable under some circumstances. Other shooters nearly fully extend the shooting-hand arm, with the support-side elbow only slightly bent. These are just guidelines, however.

Shooters using the Weaver position often report a greater level of hold stability resulting from the push-pull tension between the shooting and support hands. A similar tension can be achieved in the isosceles position, without bending the arms at the elbows and modifying the position. It should also be noted that there are "hybrid" stances that combine elements of both the Isosceles and Weaver positions. These stances are described in the NRA Personal Protection Outside the Home Course and its companion student text, *The NRA Guide to Personal Protection Outside The Home.*

THE LOW READY POSITION

In some shooting situations, you may not immediately go into a firing position, but may have to hold your firearm in a *ready position* for a period of time, in anticipation of use. Alternatively, after firing a number of shots, you may want to lower the gun temporaily, to rest the arm muscles, before continuing shooting. In both circumstances, a *ready position* is used. One ready position is presented in this course: the *low ready position.*

To assume the low ready position, take the proper grip on the pistol and extend the arms outward and downward at approximately a 45-degree angle. The firearm will be oriented toward a point on the ground several feet in front of you. Your knees should be slightly bent and the weight slightly forward, in anticipation of either movement or the acquisition of a full firing position. Your foot and shoulder position should reflect the firing position that you plan to assume (e.g., isosceles, Weaver, etc.).

The low ready position.

Another way of visualizing the low ready position is to adopt the shooting position and then simply lower the extended arms approximately 45 degrees downward.

The simplicity of the low ready position, and the unobstructed view it gives of the target, are two of its primary advantages. The position also permits easy assumption of the shooting position. With the arms already extended, the wrists already locked and the feet and shoulders already aligned, the gun is simply raised to eye level to acquire the sights and fire.

COMMON PISTOL SHOOTING ERRORS

In principle, shooting a pistol is simple: keep the sights aligned on the target as the trigger releases. In practice, however, shooting is a highly refined skill that takes coordination, discipline, and a great deal of practice. Moreover, there are many errors or habits that may contribute to poor shooting, without the shooter himself or herself being aware of them.

In general, pistol shooting errors may be traced to either a lack of *consistency* or a lack of *proper form*. Consistency refers to the ability to perform an action in exactly the same way, time after time. Proper form refers to the manner in which an act, such as aiming, holding the pistol or pulling the trigger, is performed. While some shooters who use poor form, but use it consistently, may still be able to shoot well under some circumstances, proper form is still preferable because it allows the shooter to more easily achieve or maintain consistency, accuracy, recoil control and so forth.

Note that in the following discussion, the changes in group position produced by various errors are described as they would occur for a right-handed shooter. A left-handed shooter would experience changes in the opposite direction. Note also that some shooting errors will be more evident from a one-handed shooting position.

This wide, random pattern is typical of a novice pistol shooter who lacks consistency in virtually every aspect of technique. A more experienced shooter usually succeeds in achieving tighter grouping. Even for an inexperienced shooter, group placement may reveal a specific type of pistol shooting error.

AIMING ERRORS

Aiming errors can make it impossible to reliably hit a target. There are two basic types of sighting errors. Errors in *sight alignment* result when the proper relationship of the front and rear sights is not maintained while

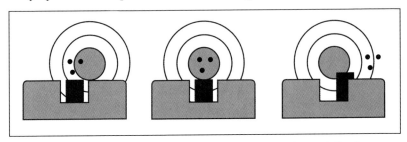

Errors in sight picture (left) and sight alignment (right) and their effects on bullet placement. Note that a sight alignment error results in greater group deviation from the desired point of impact. Proper sight picture and sight alignment are shown at center.

the shot is fired. Such errors can occur only with iron sights. Errors in *sight picture* result when the aligned iron sights, the dot of a red-dot scope, or the crosshairs of a telescopic sight, are not properly aligned with the target when the shot is fired. This most commonly happens simply because it is difficult to hold a pistol perfectly still in relation to a target.

Sight alignment errors are a greater accuracy problem than errors in sight picture. Small errors in sight picture generally cause a small shift in bullet impact. Small errors in sight alignment are magnified with greater distance, and thus produce a larger shift in bullet impact.

TRIGGER ERRORS

For maximum consistency and accuracy, the trigger of a firearm must be pressed or pulled with a uniform movement that acts in a straight rearward direction. The pull must be properly controlled to allow the sights to remain perfectly aligned with the target until the hammer, sear or firing pin is released and the shot is fired.

Poor trigger control can simply result from inconsistent application of trigger technique, or it may reflect the development of bad habits. *Jerking the trigger* may result when the shooter attempts to fire the shot at the exact instant the moving sights cross the target. Jerking the trigger invariably results in poor accuracy, as it cannot be performed with any consistency and pulls the sights out of alignment. Jerking the trigger often results in either a too-large group, or a tendency to group shots low and to

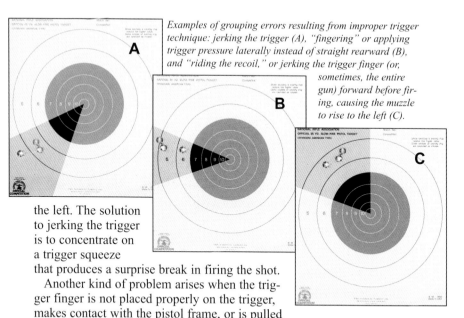

Examples of grouping errors resulting from improper trigger technique: jerking the trigger (A), "fingering" or applying trigger pressure laterally instead of straight rearward (B), and "riding the recoil," or jerking the trigger finger (or, sometimes, the entire gun) forward before firing, causing the muzzle to rise to the left (C).

the left. The solution to jerking the trigger is to concentrate on a trigger squeeze that produces a surprise break in firing the shot.

Another kind of problem arises when the trigger finger is not placed properly on the trigger, makes contact with the pistol frame, or is pulled sideways and not straight to the rear. Any of these conditions can result in lateral pressure of the trigger finger, or *fingering*. This can cause shots to deviate directly to the left of the aiming point (for a right-handed shooter).

A third type of trigger problem is produced when the shooter fails to employ a proper follow-through and instead jerks the trigger finger forward just as the shot breaks, producing a group in the 9:30 to 12:00 o'clock position. This same pattern can also be produced when the shooter, anticipating recoil, jerks the whole pistol in a recoil-like movement as the shot is fired. This is called *riding the recoil*.

Trigger problems can often be diagnosed through the use of a laser pointer attached to the firearm. Observing the movement of the laser dot when the trigger is pulled often reveals faulty trigger technique.

HOLD ERRORS

For the novice, *hold errors* result from a lack of hold control, and reflect an inability to keep the firearm still while the sights are aligned and the trigger is pulled. With any pistol held at arm's length, there will inevitably be a certain amount of movement, which will be seen in the changing relationship of the sights and the target. A beginning pistol shooter will experience a great deal of this *arc of movement*, as his or her arm muscles and nervous system are not accustomed to the challenge of holding a pistol in an extended position. One sign of a lack of hold control is an increase in group size as the shooting session progresses. Simple muscle fatigue can be made even worse when the shooter fails to rest between shots, or strings of shots. With practice, the muscles that are used in holding a pistol acquire better tone, and gun movement while aiming decreases.

GRIP ERRORS

Grip errors are errors in the way that the pistol is held. A *too-loose grip* allows excessive gun movement upon firing. Also, in the case of some semi-automatic pistols, a loose grip can lead to cycling malfunctions. A too-tight grip is also often a problem, as it is not possible to maintain a consistently hard grip for long before muscle fatigue and tremors set in.

Grip inconsistency can produce variations in the pistol's movement under recoil. This affects accuracy because the pistol begins recoiling while the bullet is still in the bore. Good grouping depends upon the bullet exiting the muzzle at the same point in the pistol's recoil pattern. A consistent grip allows this.

Ideally, the grip should allow some degree of recoil control, channeling the recoil movement in a rearward direction. Improper hand placement, and misalignment of the gun, hand, wrist and arm can cause the gun to twist or angle sideways when fired, making good grouping more difficult.

Certain grip errors produce specific group patterns. Virtually all such errors are the result of the shooter anticipating the recoil or muzzle blast of the shot. The most common of these is *breaking the wrist,* which occurs when the shooter drops the gun slightly downward at the moment the trigger is pulled in order to counteract the upward movement of the recoiling

Typical error produced by antici-pating the shot, sometimes called "breaking the wrist."

pistol. Although this dropping movement is often produced by simply breaking the wrist, it can also occur when the entire arm moves downward. Groups in the 5:30 to 6:00 o'clock area below the point of aim are often produced by breaking the wrist.

Another type of grip error, *heeling the gun,* occurs when the shooter anticipates the shot and gives the gun butt a slight push with the heel of the hand. Groups above and to the right of the point of aim are produced by this condition. *Thumbing*—applying pressure with the strong-hand thumb to the side of the gun as the shot is fired—will tend to throw groups to the side, away from the thumb (the 3 o'clock direction for a

Grouping patterns produced by several common grip errors: heeling the gun (A), thumbing (B) and lobstering, or tightening the grip as the trigger is squeezed (C).

right handed shooter). Low right grouping can be caused by another hold error, called *lobstering,* which is produced by tightening the grip as the trigger is squeezed and the shot is fired.

BREATH CONTROL ERRORS

When a person takes a breath, the abdomen, chest, shoulder girdle and arms move. Precision shooting, such as in bullseye competition, or when testing pistols from a bench, demands that gun movement be reduced to a minimum. Normally, this is done by taking a few deep breaths, letting the last breath about halfway out, and then firing the shot during a window of time about three to eight seconds after breathing stopped. This period represents the interval in which gun movement is at a minimum.

Breath control problems may occur when a shooter may simply forget to hold his or her breath during shooting, resulting in excessive gun movement during aiming, usually in rhythm with the breaths taken. Sometimes a shooter will stop breathing at the proper time, but may forget to resume breathing, or fail to take in enough air between shots to replenish the body's supply of oxygen. Lack of oxygen can result in muscle fatigue and even lightheadedness.

OTHER ERRORS

Sometimes a shooter will aim a pistol using the non-dominant eye. This often happens when a shooter is *cross-dominant* (i.e., has the dominant eye and dominant hand on different sides) and learned to shoot by using the eye and hand of the same side. In general, cross-dominant individuals should aim with the dominant eye, and hold and shoot the pistol with the non-dominant hand. For more information on determining the dominant eye, see Chapter 9: Fundamentals of Pistol Shooting Positions.

Failure to use the Natural Aiming Area (NAA) can also lead to poor shooting. In relatively static pistol sports, such as bullseye shooting, a proper NAA is important to place the body in a stable, relaxed and supportive position. In more dynamic pistol activities, such as practical pistol competition and even self-defense, shooting is often done very rapidly, almost reflexively. Using the NAA will properly index the body in relation to the target, and will make it possible to fire rapidly in a natural and efficient manner. For more information on determining a shooter's Natural Aiming Area, see Chapter 9: Fundamentals of Pistol Shooting.

Lack of proper follow-through can also lead a shooter to "give up on the shot." In this error, the shooter fails to observe the shooting fundamentals all the way through the firing of the shot, and for a few moments afterwards. In the absence of a deliberate follow-through effort, the shooter will inevitably fail, on occasion, to maintain one or more of the shooting fundamentals before the bullet leaves the muzzle.

Some errors may not relate solely to shooting technique. High-recoiling ammunition can produce any number of shooting errors, particularly in a novice shooter. Also, a broken scope sight or adjustable sight, or an inaccurate gun or ammunition can produce the appearance of shooting errors.

DIAGNOSING PISTOL SHOOTING ERRORS

Shooting errors can be diagnosed in several ways. Using a video camera to record a shooter during a range session can allow his or her form to be reviewed later, in slow-motion if necessary. When using a video camera in this way, care must be taken not to put either the camera or the camera operator in front of the firing line or the gun's muzzle. Also, as mentioned earlier, a laser mounted on the gun may also reveal these errors.

Shooters wishing to improve their pistol shooting may consult the numerous books and magazines listed in Appendix B: Information and Training Resources.

CHAPTER 14

CLEARING COMMON PISTOL STOPPAGES

Though modern repeating pistols offer far greater reliability than their predecessors, they are still machines and thus can malfunction. An occasional jam is a minor annoyance for a casual plinker, but may cost a target shooter a win, or have even more dire consequences for a person who owns a pistol for protection. Thus, the ability to quickly recognize and resolve a stoppage is a skill every pistol shooter should possess.

CAUSES OF STOPPAGES

Most pistol stoppages are related to ammunition problems, including improperly-made reloaded ammunition or, with semi-automatic pistols, factory ammunition too weak to cycle the action. Some semi-automatics also are finicky regarding the feeding of different bullet shapes and cartridge lengths, so various loads may have to be tested to find one that fires and functions reliably in a particular gun. Persistent reliability problems may indicate a gun problem that must be addressed by a gunsmith.

Stoppages can also be caused when the gun is dirty, rusty, poorly-maintained, or simply worn or damaged through frequent use (see Chapter 15: Cleaning and Maintaining Your Pistol). Always follow the manufacturer's recommendations regarding the replacement of parts that can wear out or fatigue, such as recoil springs.

FAILURE TO FIRE

A *failure to fire* occurs whenever the hammer or firing pin falls on a loaded chamber (or what is thought to be a loaded chamber) and the gun does not fire. This type of stoppage can occur with any kind of pistol.

With a revolver, a failure to fire can occur when all the cartridges in the cylinder have been fired, or when the hammer has fallen on an empty chamber. Similarly, when a semi-automatic pistol fails to load the top cartridge in the magazine into the chamber, a failure to fire can take place when the hammer or firing pin falls on an empty chamber.

If the hammer or firing pin of a pistol falls on a live cartridge and fails to fire it, the most common problem is the ammunition used—a "dud" cartridge, a hangfire or misfire (see Chapter 8: Ammunition Fundamentals).

The recommended procedure is to wait 30 to 60 seconds with the muzzle pointed downrange, in the event that the condition you are experiencing is a hangfire. In situations in which this is not practical, as in a defensive encounter, the shooter should simply pull the trigger again, if that is possible with the particular pistol. With a revolver, this will bring a fresh (and hopefully functioning) cartridge in line with the firing pin. With a double-action semi-automatic, a second firing pin hit on the primer may discharge the cartridge.

A faint firing pin indentation (left case) can result in a failure to fire, and may indicate a problem with the pistol.

A persistent failure-to-fire problem, especially when good-quality factory ammunition is used, may indicate a problem with the pistol, such as a broken firing pin. Examination of the primers of both the functioning and non-functioning cartridges for proper firing-pin indentation could reveal if this is the case. Generally, a failure-to-fire condition that is not ammunition-related requires the attention of a gunsmith.

SPECIFIC SEMI-AUTOMATIC PISTOL STOPPAGES

Failure to Go into Battery. This stoppage occurs when the slide does not return all the way forward and the cartridge is not fully seated in the chamber. Usually the slide is left about 1/8" to 1/4" short of going into battery.

Most commonly this type of stoppage is caused by a round that gets jammed on the feed ramp leading into the chamber, or by an oversize or over-length cartridge. On occasion, failure to go into battery can also be produced by an excessively dirty chamber.

Failure to go into battery. Note overhang at the rear of the slide.

Failure to eject, as evidenced by empty case in ejection port.

Failure to Eject. In this condition, the fired case is extracted at least partially from the chamber, but is not completely ejected from the pistol. The fired case may remain inside the slide, possibly becoming jammed into the chamber, or it may be partially protruding from the ejection port, a condition known as a *stovepipe* stoppage.

Tap, Rack and Assess Drill

Just about all semi-automatic pistols can be cleared of all three of the above stoppages—failure to go into battery, failure to fire, and failure to eject—using a single immediate action drill consisting of three steps, referred to as *tap, rack* and *assess.*

When a stoppage occurs, your trigger finger should be removed from the trigger. Next, *tap* the base of the magazine with the palm of the support

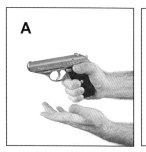

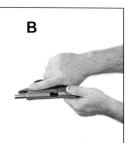

hand to ensure it is fully seated (A). Then, invert the pistol by rotating toward the thumb of the shooting hand, and *rack* the slide vigorously by pulling it all the way to the rear (B) and releasing it to go forward under spring tension. Inverting the pistol before racking the slide and shaking the gun while the slide is held fully back will dislodge all but the most stubborn empty case or jammed cartridge. Finally, reassume the shooting position, *assess* the target area downrange, and resume firing, if appropriate (C).

SPECIFIC REVOLVER STOPPAGES

Failure to Eject Cases from the Cylinder. Difficulty in ejecting fired cases from a revolver cylinder may result from oversized or high-pressure cartridges, dirt in the chambers or roughly machined chambers. When rapid reloading is necessary, the action to be taken to overcome this is to hit the ejector rod again with greater force. Be careful to strike in a straight line with the rod to prevent bending it with an off-axis strike. If this problem is encountered during practice sessions, a gunsmith's assistance should be sought to eliminate it.

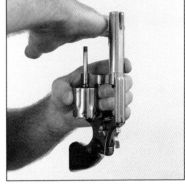

If the first strike of the ejector rod fails to eject all the cases, strike it again with greater force, in a straight line to prevent bending the rod.

PART IV

PISTOL MAINTENANCE, SELECTION AND USE

CHAPTER 15

CLEANING AND MAINTAINING YOUR PISTOL

NO AMMUNITION IN THE GUN CLEANING AREA.

A gun that is regularly fired accumulates dirt, powder residue and other foreign matter, all of which can make it more prone to stoppage, wear and corrosion. Even a firearm that is left untouched on a shelf or in a drawer can accumulate sufficient dust and dirt to affect functioning. Responsible gun owners understand that removing such material is critical to ensure gun reliability and readiness. A gun that is properly maintained at regular intervals—including regular cleaning, inspection and lubrication, as well as a periodic gunsmith check-up—will function more reliably, shoot more accurately and last longer than one whose care is neglected.

Every gun owner should have a gun cleaning kit consisting of:
- cloth patches,
- a cleaning rod and cleaning rod attachments, including a bore brush and tips to hold patches,
- a small brush (for cleaning gun crevices),
- gun solvent (bore cleaner),
- gun oil, and
- a soft cloth.

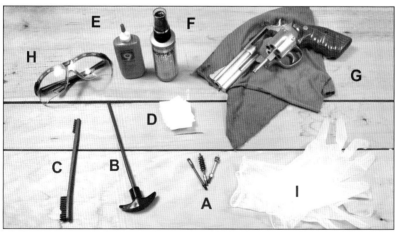

The components of a basic gun cleaning kit, including (A) a bore brush and jags for holding cleaning patches, (B) a cleaning rod, (C) a small brush, (D) cotton cleaning patches, (E) gun oil, (F) gun cleaning solvent, (G) a soft cloth, and (H) eye protection. Also shown are thin rubber gloves (I), which may help protect the skin from dirt, oil and solvent.

Kits containing all or most of these items are commercially available at any gun shop and many hardware, sporting goods and large discount stores. Make sure that any such kit, or any individual cleaning rod, jag (a tip designed specifically to hold a cleaning patch) or bore brush is the proper size for your pistol's caliber. Also, select patches of the proper size.

Additionally, you need safety glasses to protect your eyes from cleaning solvents and spring-loaded parts that may be inadvertently released from your gun. Also recommended are thin rubber gloves to protect your skin from exposure to solvents, lubricants, firing residues and lead particles. Be sure that your gun-cleaning area has good ventilation, and do not eat, drink or smoke while performing firearm cleaning or maintenance.

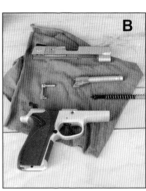

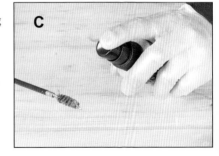

The first step in cleaning your firearm is to ensure that it is unloaded (A). **No ammunition should be in the cleaning area.**

Next, disassemble your firearm according to the instructions in the owner's manual for the gun (B). If you do not have an owner's manual, you can usually obtain one from your gun's manufacturer. Also, a professional gunsmith may be able to show you how to disassemble your gun.

Attach the bore brush to the cleaning rod and moisten it with gun cleaning solvent (C). If possible, use a dropper or spray to put solvent onto the brush; avoid dipping the brush in the solvent, as this contaminates the clean solvent with dirt and grit that may be on the brush. Push the brush all the way through the bore from the chamber

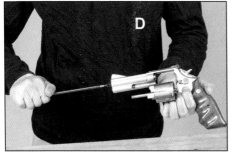

whenever possible, then pull it back through (D). Do not try to reverse direction with the brush still in the bore. Run the brush through the bore about 10-15 times, adding solvent to it as necessary.

Attach the jag to the cleaning rod (E) and push a patch moistened with solvent through the bore (F). This patch will come out quite dirty with the material that was loosened by the solvent and the bore brush. Run several dry patches through the bore. These should come out progressively clean-

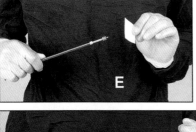

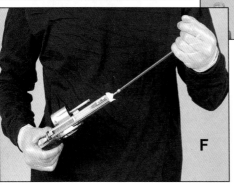

er, until virtually no fouling is visible. If the patches keep coming out somewhat dirty, repeat the cleaning process as outlined above. Visually check the bore for any remaining fouling, lead, or powder residue.

In cleaning a revolver, the cylinders are cleaned with the bore brush and patches using much the same technique as is employed in cleaning the bore (G).

Once the bore is clean, residue must be removed from other gun surfaces. Use a solvent-soaked patch, cotton swab or toothbrush, as appropriate, to loosen and remove powder residue and other matter from working surfaces (H). On a semi-automatic pistol, such surfaces include the interior of the slide, the slide and frame rails, and the exterior barrel surface. On a

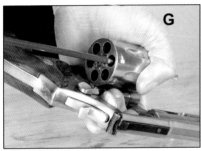

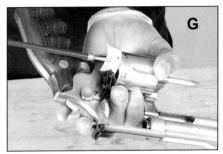

revolver, such surfaces include the crane, frame, and any action parts that are accessed by the removal of the stocks. Finally, reassemble the pistol and wipe it with a soft, lightly oiled cloth (I).

Maintenance of semi-automatic pistol magazines is critical for proper pistol functioning. Most magazines are designed to be disassembled; instructions should be in your owner's manual. Once the magazine is disassembled, remove dirt and powder residue from the inside of the magazine body using a brush and patches (J).

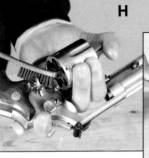

In most cases, the owner's manual will present only basic disassembly instructions for general cleaning and maintenance; further gun disassembly by the owner is usually discouraged. However, dirt and powder residue collects in interior action areas that can be accessed only by complete disassembly. A partial cleaning of these inaccessible areas may be achieved by flushing the action with gun cleaner or a solvent that leaves no residue, such as brake cleaner. The solvent is sprayed into the action in such a way as to allow the excess to drain freely (such as with the stocks removed), dissolving and flushing away loosened dirt and residue.

INSPECTING YOUR FIREARM

The ideal time for giving your firearm a thorough visual inspection is when it is disassembled after cleaning. Defects are easiest to spot on parts that are free of dirt, residue and oil. Look for cracks, burred, pitted or indented areas, broken components and so forth. Also be aware of screws or pins that have worked loose, sights that have drifted from recoil forces, or parts that seem to have shifted from their normal positions.

Additionally, every time you pick up your firearm, whether to practice at the range, dry-fire in your basement, or clean it in your workroom, you should give it a cursory inspection (after, of course, making sure it is unloaded). Look for the buildup of firing residues; grips screws or other parts that have become loose; excessive oil leaking out of the joints between parts; and any other condition that may affect the functioning of the gun. Getting in the habit of making this kind of inspection will help you determine when cleaning or lubrication is necessary, or if there are any conditions that may make your gun unsafe or unreliable.

LUBRICATING YOUR FIREARM

Cleaning powder residues and other foreign material from the gun usually removes necessary lubrication from working surfaces. Thus, it is essential to re-lubricate the firearm after it has been cleaned.

The owner's manual for your gun will likely contain detailed instructions on the proper method of lubrication. In general, lubricate revolvers in the areas of the crane, ejector rod, and cylinder latch, and around the sides of the hammer and trigger. With the stocks removed, you may also squirt oil into action areas to smooth the trigger pull.

Semi-automatic pistols should be lubricated on the slide and frame rails, at the muzzle (where the barrel engages the slide), and in the barrel locking area. Also apply a small amount of oil to the sides of the trigger and hammer where they enter the frame, and drip a little lubricant into action areas. If you desire, you may put a very light film of oil on the exterior surface of the magazines to prevent rust.

It is critical not to allow oil to be transferred to the cartridges carried within the magazine. Oil on cartridge cases can penetrate to the primer, making its ignition unreliable, and may have other harmful effects on gun functioning as well.

Use only those lubricants designed expressly for use in firearms. Over time, improper lubricants may become gummy, impairing proper gun functioning, or may be too thin or runny to provide lasting protection. Also, firearms that are used in climates that are extremely hot, cold, wet or dusty

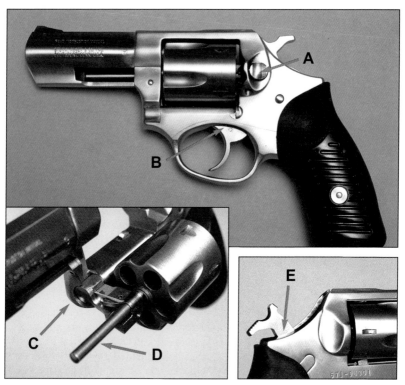

Lubrication points for a revolver include the cylinder latch (A), the junction of the trigger and the frame (B), the crane (C), the ejector rod (D), and alongside the hammer where it meets the frame (E). With the hammer back, a few drops of oil may also be dripped into the action to lubricate internal action parts. Internal parts may also be accessed for lubrication by removing the stocks.

often have very special lubrication needs, as do firearms that will be stored for extended periods. Consult with a gun shop or gunsmith to determine the proper lubricants to be used with your firearm.

It is also important to avoid over-lubricating your pistol, or leaving oil in certain areas. For example, while a thin film of oil should coat the bore of a firearm that is to be stored, all oil should be removed from the bore before the gun is fired. Excess lubricant can also penetrate wood stocks and cause them to deteriorate. Too much oil left on the exterior of a pistol that is carried in a leather holster can soak into the leather, softening it. This can be of particular concern with leather holsters that are molded to snugly fit a particular pistol model. As explained above, oil left inside the magazine of a semi-automatic pistol or the chambers of a revolver cylinder can contaminate cartridge primers and lead to misfires.

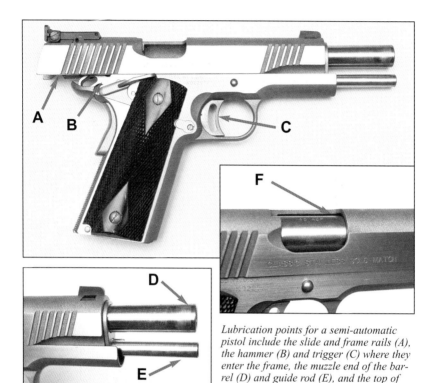

Lubrication points for a semi-automatic pistol include the slide and frame rails (A), the hammer (B) and trigger (C) where they enter the frame, the muzzle end of the barrel (D) and guide rod (E), and the top of the chamber end of the barrel (F).

FUNCTION CHECKING YOUR FIREARM

After cleaning, inspecting and lubricating the firearm, the final stage is reassembly and function checking. The inspection process referred to previously should continue during reassembly. Be aware of parts that do not go together as they should, a sudden increase in the play or looseness of pins and other components, and so forth.

When the firearm is reassembled, make sure that it is unloaded and then dry-fire it a few times to see if there are any changes in the feel of the trigger or the functioning of the controls. With a revolver, swing the cylinder out and test the action of the extractor rod. Rack the slide of a semiautomatic and ensure that its various safety controls are functioning. Don't just look with your eyes; listen with your ears. Sometimes the sound of the gun as it is cycled or dry-fired can reveal a functional problem.

Similarly, when firing live ammunition at the range, be aware of any changes in the gun's function or feel. Gradual changes in gun function such as sluggish cycling, frequent stoppages or larger groups can result from a buildup of dirt, powder residue, congealed lubricant and so forth. Thorough cleaning and lubrication often restores proper functioning in such cases. However, a sudden tendency of the gun to misfire, jam, or change the size or location of its groups may be a sign of a broken part or other serious mechanical problem that usually requires gunsmith attention.

OTHER MAINTENANCE

Firearm maintenance involves more than just cleaning, inspection, lubrication and function testing. Both semi-automatic pistols and revolvers are powered by springs, which can, over time, fatigue. The springs that power revolver hammers generally last for many years, however, revolvers having a tendency to produce light hits on the primer may be suffering from weak springs.

Recoil springs on semi-automatic pistols should be regularly replaced, usually every several thousand rounds. Your owner's manual should have specific recommendations regarding recoil spring replacement, as well as directions for installing new springs. Magazine springs, too, sometimes require replacement, as some will lose stiffness over time (particularly when left compressed) and produce feeding problems. A competent gunsmith can diagnose and remedy problems stemming from fatigued springs.

Performing regular mainte-nance, such as the replacement of fatigued recoil springs (above), is a part of responsible firearm ownership.

GUNSMITH CHECK-UP

In addition to the normal maintenance you can perform, it is important to periodically have a gunsmith completely disassemble, clean, inspect and lubricate your firearm. This is also an opportunity for an experienced eye to look for wear, breakage or other conditions that may affect your gun's ability to function properly.

The frequency of this kind of gunsmith examination depends upon your shooting habits. In general, if you practice regularly with your firearm, an annual check-up is recommended.

CHAPTER 16

SELECTING PISTOLS, PISTOL AMMUNITION AND ACCESSORIES

Today's pistol buyer has an unprecedented range of choices of pistol manufacturers, models, action types and calibers, not to mention ammunition and accessories. This can be confusing, especially for the first-time gun buyer. For such an individual, a logical selection process is needed.

SELECTING A PISTOL

Stage 1: Research

Before the research process is even started, the following question should be answered by anyone thinking of buying a pistol: *Am I a sufficiently responsible person to own a firearm?* While gun ownership is a Constitutionally-guaranteed right, there are still those who lack the maturity, emotional stability, or willingness to accept the responsibility of gun ownership. Anyone who recognizes this in him- or herself, and chooses not to own a firearm, should be commended for their responsible decision.

For those who elect to own a pistol, the single most important selection criterion revolves around the *purpose* of the firearm. In some cases, there will be a single clear-cut reason for pistol ownership—formal target shooting, hunting, or self-defense, for example. The identification of this reason greatly simplifies pistol selection.

Many shooters, however, intend to use a pistol for a number of activities, such as target shooting, plinking and self-defense. Generally, any claim that one pistol will do everything should be met with skepticism. Most multipurpose pistols embody a series of compromises that may make them mediocre, at best, for any single function. The shooter wishing to engage in several different shooting activities will usually end up with a separate gun for each activity, or a single gun that is best suited for the highest-priority purpose.

The *action type* of the desired pistol should also be selected in this stage. Sometimes the action type will be determined by the purpose. Cowboy

Action shooters, for example, will usually select a single-action revolver. For most other activities, the choice will be between a semi-automatic pistol or a double-action revolver. The semi-automatic has the edge in concealability, cartridge capacity (as many as 18 to 20 rounds) and speed of reloading, while the revolver offers simpler operation and greater reliability. A revolver is also preferable for shooters lacking mechanical aptitude.

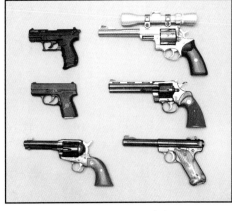

Pistols for different purposes, including concealed carry, hunting, and bullseye, Cowboy Action and silhouette competition.

The prospective gun buyer, in the research stage, should also look into the reputation of the manufacturer and model of any pistol under consideration. Usually, the best choice is a standard model of proven design, made by an established, reputable gunmaker. Newly-introduced or innovative designs from new gun companies should probably be avoided.

The pistol's materials may also influence pistol selection. At one time all guns were made of steel and wood; now, titanium and aluminum alloys, as well as polymer materials, are commonplace. As a general rule, steel is still the strongest material, but most pistol owners will not shoot enough to see a difference in longevity between steel and any other material. Steel is also heavy and can corrode, while aluminum alloys and polymers do not corrode to any appreciable extent. Because of their light weight, titanium, aluminum and polymer materials are often used in carry pistols. There is a downside to such materials, however. Lightweight guns are easy to carry, but give more recoil than heavier, all-steel firearms of the same size.

A final, crucial factor to be researched is *safety*. While modern firearms from reputable manufacturers are generally over-engineered, with multiple safety features built in, some designs may confer an additional margin of safety in certain situations, such as in households in which there are children or others not authorized to use or handle the firearm. Both revolvers and semi-automatic pistols can have a variety of safety features; such as manual safety levers, magazine disconnectors, grip safeties, and even key-operated action locks. The prospective gun buyer should weigh the merits of such features in light of his or her own particular living situation. Some safety features may compromise rapid pistol deployment in an emergency situation.

As a general rule, the novice pistol owner is best with a new firearm having a full warranty, rather than a used model whose previous history of use or abuse may be unknown. An exception might be made for a used pistol sold and warranted by a reputable gun dealer.

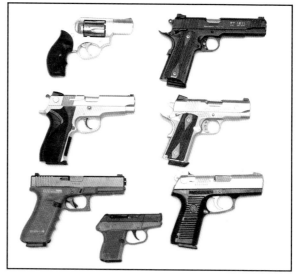

Modern pistols may be made completely of steel (top row), or have frames of aluminum (middle row) or or polymer materials (bottom row).

A variety of information resources can be consulted in the research phase, including books, magazines, gun dealers, gun clubs and the internet (see Appendix B: Information and Training Resources).

Stage II: Examination

Once the research stage has narrowed the range of choices down to a dozen models or fewer, the prospective gun buyer should examine these choices in a gun shop.

Here, the shooter may learn much about each model—how it feels in the hand, how large and heavy it is, the ease with which the controls may be manipulated and so forth. With the help of a knowledgeable store clerk, the gun buyer can go through the operations required to load, unload, and fire the firearm, using an empty gun.

Gun fit is an important factor in pistol selection, and is largely subjective. Small differences in grip shape, thickness and angle, and even barrel length and slide weight may radically alter the feel of the gun in the hand. Ideally, the *trigger reach*—the distance from the backstrap of the frame to the trigger face—should allow the trigger finger to engage the trigger somewhere from the middle of the pad of the fingertip to the first joint. Small-handed persons often have difficulty with pistol grips that are too thick or a trigger that is too far forward, or may have problems in reaching all the pistol's controls. This is a particular problem with high-capacity semi-automatic pistols. Most such persons are better off with small- to medium-frame semi-automatics and revolvers. Less commonly, a large-handed person will encounter a small pocket or defensive pistol having a too-small grip or trigger guard, or controls too small for easy manipulation.

Also important is the physical strength required to operate the pistol. Many people have difficulty retracting the slide of a semi-automatic pistol with a stiff recoil spring. Some persons may also lack the finger strength to pull the trigger of a double-action revolver. Pistols vary in recoil spring stiffness and trigger pull weight, so a prospective gun buyer should try many different models.

Cost and quality are also factors. While low-price models may be appealing, they can represent false economy if they fail to provide the desired reliability, durability or accuracy. The price and availability of ammunition, parts, accessories and so forth should also be considered. Also, certain models are supplied with a greater number of aftermarket parts and accessories, or may be easier for a gunsmith to work on.

Through the process outlined above in Stage II, the prospective gun buyer should be able to further narrow the number of potential choices.

Stage III: Test Firing

The final stage in the pistol selection process involves test firing representative samples of the remaining viable choices. This often may be accomplished at ranges having a variety of pistols for rent. In this activity, the individual can judge the recoil, accuracy, comfort and feel of each. Any stoppages or other problems can be noted.

Semi-automatic pistols should be fired with one- and two-hand holds, with both a tight and a loose grip, and with the gun held in various positions—upright, sideways and upside-down. The shooter should note the trajectory of the fired brass; ejected shells should land around five to six feet away. Loads of different levels of power and with different bullet shapes should also be tried.

Revolvers should be fired with loads of different power levels, in both the single-action and (if applicable) double-action modes. With all loads, fired cases should easily eject from all cylinders.

  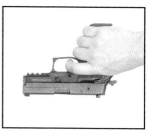

Test firing of semi-automatic pistols should involve various firing orientations.

With all pistol types, firing pin indentations should be deep and round, whether the firearm is fired in the single-action or double-action mode (if applicable). Recoil and accuracy should be evaluated with various loads. Adjustable sights should be evaluated to ensure that sight adjustments are crisp and accurate. Fixed-sight guns should be tested to note the degree of deviation of the bullet impacts from the point of aim.

Fired cases should show deep primer indentations (right) rather than light indentations.

Finally, the test firing session will help the gun buyer determine the appropriate caliber to buy. Many gun designs are produced in similar models in several chamberings, such as 9 mm Para, .40 S&W and .45 ACP. Thus, in many cases, a new gun buyer may decide upon a specific pistol design, and have the further choice of a variety of chamberings, with different levels of recoil.

SELECTING PISTOL AMMUNITION AND ACCESSORIES

Accuracy, reliability and other aspects of pistol performance depend at least as much upon the ammunition chosen as on the particular gun design. Also, even after the proper gun and ammunition are chosen, a variety of pistol accessories can further enhance a shooter's enjoyment and performance in any shooting activity.

Selecting Pistol Ammunition

The selection of the proper ammunition type and load involves consideration of several factors, among the most important of which are: *safety, purpose, reliability, accuracy,* and *recoil.*

Safety. Ammunition safety primarily involves using the proper ammunition for the firearm. As described in Chapter 8: Ammunition Fundamentals, this is accomplished by matching the caliber designation on the barrel and/or slide with that on the ammunition package and cartridge headstamp. Additionally, higher-pressure "+P" and "+P+" loads should be used only in those firearms certified for them.

As a general rule, the novice pistol owner should avoid reloaded ammunition, as well as military surplus ammunition, and purchase only new ammunition from a reputable manufacturer.

Purpose. The intended purpose of the pistol/ammunition combination is the main factor in determining the choice of caliber, cartridge power, and bullet weight, design and construction. For example, target shooting, hunting and self-defense all require different types of ammunition.

Information on the general ammunition types required for different pistol shooting activities can be found in many gun books, magazines and videos, as are listed in Appendix B: Information and Training Resources.

Reliability. Reliability is the ability of a load to consistently feed, fire, eject and cycle the action. Factors that may influence ammunition reliability include load power, bullet shape, cartridge overall length, crimp and much more. In general, any load used in a critical application should be absolutely reliable during a test of 200 to as many as 500 rounds.

Persistent reliability problems with various loads may indicate a situation that must require resolution by a gunsmith.

Accuracy. Accuracy is a function of several factors: the gun, the load used, and the skill of the shooter. The level of accuracy required in different activities can vary greatly. Information on the accuracy needed in various pistol shooting activities can be found in various books, magazines and videos (see Appendix B: Information and Training Resources).

Accuracy testing should ideally involve a number of five-shot groups fired from a bench-rest position at a target placed at an appropriate distance (see Chapter 11: The Benchrest Position).

Recoil. The recoil or "kick" felt by the shooter upon firing a gun will vary with gun weight, cartridge power, bullet weight, grip size and shape, and more. Additionally, shooters differ in their sensitivity to recoil. Excessive recoil can inhibit the ability to quickly fire multiple accurate shots, and can produce a flinch reflex that impairs accuracy. Determining the recoil a shooter can tolerate is usually made by test-firing different guns in different calibers. Novice shooters should avoid hard-kicking pistols, as early exposure to high levels of recoil can cause flinching, shot anticipation, jerking the trigger and other unwanted habits. Note that many cartridges come in several loads that may vary greatly in recoil.

Selecting Pistol Accessories

Various types of pistol accessories can add greatly to one's enjoyment of any pistol shooting activity, as well as contributing to better shooting performance.

Eye and *hearing protection* are perhaps the most important accessories a shooter must have (see Chapter 1: Basic Firearm Safety).

A *range bag* of leather, canvas or nylon allows convenient carry and storage of the pistol, ammunition, eye and hearing protection, targets and more. Although the pistol may be carried loosely in the range bag, a *pistol rug* or *pistol box* is usually preferable. The latter has the advantage of being lockable with a padlock, and thus provides some security when transporting or storing the firearm.

Also for inclusion in the range bag is a small *tool kit* containing, at a minimum, the items used for disassembling the pistol. A basic *cleaning kit* may be included (see Chapter 15: Cleaning and Maintaining Your Pistol).

Other items for the range bag are a small *first aid kit*, a *stapler* for mounting targets on the target frame and a recoil-absorbing *shooting glove.*

For semi-automatic pistols, additional *magazines* are mandatory, as they can be easily damaged, even in normal use. Factory or high-quality after-market magazines should be favored over inexpensive "no-name" units, which may not function properly. Note that some pistols function better with one brand of magazine than another. Loading high-capacity semi-automatic pistol magazines to full capacity is made easier with another accessory, the *magazine loader.* For revolvers, *speedloaders* make reloading faster and easier.

A *holster* is essential for concealed carry or hunting purposes, and may also be convenient when shooting at a range or in an outdoor environment.

Holsters come in many different styles and materials, with carry holsters being different in design from hunting and general-purpose models. Also useful, for some purposes, are *holster belts* and *magazine* or *speedloader pouches*. Information on selecting a carry holster can be found in the NRA Personal Protection Outside the Home Course and its companion textbook, the *NRA Guide to the Basics of Personal Protection Outside the Home*.

Many pistol accessories take the form of *aftermarket parts*, which can improve a pistol's ergonomics and accuracy, decrease recoil, or enhance controllability. Examples of such parts include sights, triggers, match-grade barrels, springs and different grips or stocks. A gunsmith should be consulted regarding the selection and installation of any such parts.

Pistol targets come in a variety of sizes, shapes and colors. While pistol competitors will use the targets of their particular discipline, recreational shooters have a variety of targets for practice, testing and plinking. *Target pasters* cover bullet holes in the target, extending target life.

Various pistol accessories, including range bag, pistol rug, holster magazine pouches, and, magazine loader.

Depending upon the shooting activity, other accessories may also be useful. A *spotting scope* allows bullet holes to be seen in a distant target; a *chronograph* measures bullet muzzle velocity, which is crucial to the calculation of bullet energy and trajectory; and a *shooting timer* is used for shooting practice or competitions conducted under time limits.

CHAPTER 17

PISTOL SHOOTING ACTIVITIES AND OPPORTUNITIES FOR SKILL DEVELOPMENT

In general, there are four main uses to which a firearm may be put: *recreational shooting*, *hunting*, *target competition*, and *self-defense*. Despite claims to the contrary by those seeking to further restrict their ownership, pistols are commonly employed for all of these activities.

RECREATIONAL SHOOTING

Although many thousands of shooters own pistols for hunting, for formal target shooting, or for self-defense, by far the greatest number of shots fired from pistols each year involve casual recreational shooting, often called *plinking*. Plinking is quite simply the name given to any form of

Recreational shooting, or "plinking," involves any safe, legal informal target shooting.

informal target shooting, done with any type of pistol at any type of safe target. The only limitations placed on this activity are those imposed by safety, legal restrictions, and the shooter's imagination.

Plinking can be done at a dedicated indoor or outdoor range facility, or on private or public land (subject to applicable local, state and federal laws). Indoor pistol ranges are fairly common, and are often found near large metropolitan areas in states and local jurisdictions that permit citizens to own pistols. Shooting ranges can usually be found by looking in the yellow pages of the local phone book, or by asking a local gun shop.

Each range will have rules dealing with safety, permissible shooting positions, drawing from holsters, caliber restrictions and so forth. Some ranges may have a Range Safety Officer on duty. Every shooter is responsible for learning and observing all range rules.

Some shooters may prefer to shoot on public or private land rather than a range. In such situations, however, safety is even more of a concern. The shooter must be responsible for always pointing the pistol in a safe direction, establishing a proper backstop, ensuring that unauthorized persons do not wander into the line of fire and so forth. The safety rule "Know Your Target and What is Beyond" is particularly important, as a bullet from even a .22 rimfire may travel a mile or more from a pistol fired when pointing skyward. Shooters must also be good stewards of the land, not trespassing on private property, removing all their spent cases and trash, and avoiding improper targets, such as glass bottles, old batteries, etc.

Pistol owners may use recreational shooting to sharpen their skills for hunting, target shooting or self-defense; most often, however, the emphasis is simply on fun. While standard bullseye targets are extremely popular, other types of targets--many in vogue decades ago--including those consisting of small dots (used for "dot shooting"), playing card decks (used to shoot poker hands), are also used. In the absence of a printed target, challenges may be improvised. For example, a piece of 8 1/2" by 11" piece of paper may be put out at 10 yards or so, and a single bullet hole put somewhere on the sheet. Each successive shooter must attempt to place his or her shot as close as possible to the original bullet hole.

In addition to a gun and ammunition, recreational shooting usually requires additional gear, such as a shooting bag, cleaning kit, tool kit and, of course, eye and ear protection.

Finally, recreational shooting is the best way to introduce a new shooter to pistol shooting, and to ingrain the rules of safety and the principles of good marksmanship in a relaxed and friendly atmosphere.

PISTOL HUNTING

The claim that pistols have no sporting use is easily disproven by the several million hunters who use pistols to harvest everything from birds and squirrels to big-game such as deer, elk, moose and bear. Using specialized single-shot pistols or highly powerful revolvers, some intrepid hunters have even humanely taken dangerous African game.

There are basically three types of pistol hunting activities: *small game hunting and pest control* (involving game such as squirrels, rabbits and crows), *varmint hunting* (involving game such as prairie dogs, groundhogs and coyotes), and *big-game hunting* (involving deer-sized and larger animals). Each type of hunting involves different types of firearms, ammunition and accessories, as well as different shooting skills.

Pistol hunting typically involves skill in stalking, marksmanship and woodsmanship.

Some jurisdictions have certain requirements for hunting pistols, such as a minimum muzzle energy for pistols used for deer-size game, or limitations on the capacity of magazines for semi-automatic hunting pistols. Almost all jurisdictions mandate every hunter to have a hunting license, usually issued upon successful completion of a hunter education course.

Regulations regarding hunting on public or private lands are usually readily available from the state fish and game service or other similar office.

Advice on the selection of pistols, ammunition and accessories for a particular type of hunting can be obtained from a variety of sources, including local gun shops, gun clubs, hunting guides or outfitters, videos and DVDs, books, hunting websites on the internet, and hunting-oriented magazines such as *The American Hunter*.

TARGET SHOOTING

Many pistol owners participate in various types of target competition, sometimes simply to sharpen their skills for other shooting activities. There are far too many pistol target shooting sports to discuss all of them here. The vast majority of pistol target shooters compete in one or more of four main activities: *bullseye shooting, practical pistol shooting, silhouette shooting* and *cowboy action shooting.*

Bullseye Competition

Bullseye pistol shooting is conducted using a one-hand hold. Firing is generally at round targets, called *bullseyes*, with a series of concentric scoring rings. Most bullseye shooting is normally conducted in a relatively slow, deliberate manner, with a high premium placed on accuracy.

NRA conventional pistol (bullseye) competition consists of slow-, timed- and rapid-fire strings fired at bullseye targets which can be set from 50 feet to 50 yards. Four general types of pistols are used in NRA conventional pistol competition: the .45 Caliber Pistol, Service Pistol, Center-Fire Pistol, and .22-Caliber Pistol. Additionally, the Distinguished Revolver category specifies the use of a factory .38 Special Revolver. In some bullseye matches, the competitor will fire three different types of guns—the .45 caliber

NRA bullseye shooting generally involves several types of guns. Here are shown a .22 pistol, .45-cal. pistol, and a .38 Spl. revolver.

pistol, center-fire pistol, and .22 caliber pistol. Red-dot sights are allowed, and light target loads are usually favored, although standard-power .45 ACP ammunition is required in certain matches for the .45 caliber pistol. *International Pistol* competition is practiced worldwide, and is featured in the Olympics. Five types of pistols are utilized in this type of competition. *Free pistols* are specialized .22 Long Rifle sin-

All bullseye shooting is done using a one-handed standing position. Many disciplines allow the use of red-dot sights, as shown.

gle-shot arms with very light triggers and iron sights. Free pistol competition is very exacting, with the 10-ring of the 50-meter free pistol target being only 50 mm (slightly more than 2") in diameter. The *rapid-fire pistol* is a semi-automatic or revolver in .22 Long Rifle, designed for a course of fire featuring five turning targets exposed for only a few seconds, during which time one shot is placed on each target. The *international center-fire pistol* can be an iron-sighted semi-automatic or revolver in any caliber from .30 caliber to .38 caliber. The *standard pistol* and *women's sport pistol* are similar to the center-fire pistol, but are chambered for .22 Long Rifle ammunition. Finally, *international air pistol* competition is limited to .177" air pistols with iron sights. All air pistol competition is conducted at 10 meters.

Typical accessories for all forms of bullseye shooting include a spotting scope and stand, ammunition blocks, and a pistol box that can hold several pistols as well as the spotting scope and ammunition.

To contact the sanctioning bodies for these forms of bullseye competition, see Appendix B: Information and Training Resources.

Practical Pistol Competition

The various pistol shooting sports known collectively as *practical pistol competition* were originally derived from the training regimen of the Mexican Federales, which utilized life-size silhouette targets, a two-handed shooting grip, and rapid multiple-target engagement at relatively close

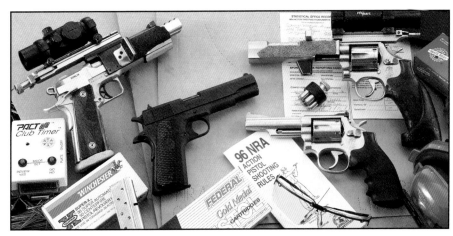

NRA Action Pistol shooting is a type of practical pistol competition requiring accuracy, consistency and speed. The Action Pistol guns shown here range from highly specialized pistols (top row) to stock revolvers and semi-automatics.

range. Practical pistol shooting is generally done "from the leather," by drawing a gun from a holster. Targets are fairly large—cardboard silhouettes with embossed scoring rings, or steel plates of various sizes and shapes—and close, most set at 25 yards or less. Some sports utilize *Comstock scoring*, in which both the point value of the hits, as well as the total elapsed time to shoot the stage, are used to compute the score.

International Practical Shooting Confederation (IPSC) and *International Defensive Pistol Association (IDPA)* competition are similar in many respects. Both employ humanoid cardboard targets; both utilize Comstock scoring; and both employ ever-changing target arrays, rather than standard courses of fire, to challenge competitors' problem-solving skills. While "race guns" with compensators and red-dot sights are allowed in IPSC's Open class, they are forbidden in IDPA competition, which stresses defensive guns, tactics and shooting scenarios. IDPA offers classes for most types

NRA Action Pistol shooting involves a number of unique courses of fire, such as the Falling Plate event.

of stock and custom defensive semi-automatics and revolvers.

NRA Action Pistol competition, like IPSC and IDPA shooting, starts from the holster. However, this sport utilizes a number of standardized stages, and each string is usually fired under time limits rather than Comstock scoring.

Because of its ergonomics, light and crisp trigger pull, robust design and virtually unlimited potential for customization, pistols of the M1911A1 design are

Police Practical Competition (PPC) tests shooting skills relevant to law-enforcement. Here competitors shoot at B-27 targets at extended range.

the most popular in IPSC, IDPA and Action Pistol events. However, other makes of semi-automatic pistols, as well as revolvers, are also popular, particularly in IDPA matches, which have separate classes for such pistols.

Popular practical pistol calibers include 9mm Para, .38 Super, .40 S&W and .45 ACP. Practical pistol sports commonly require loads that meet a minimum *power factor*, calculated by multiplying bullet weight in grains by muzzle velocity in feet per second, and dividing by 1,000. Minimum power factors for various practical pistol sports range from 120 to 165.

Bull-barreled revolvers are preferred in a fourth type of practical pistol shooting, *Police Practical Competition (PPC)*, although the sport also has

Many PPC competitors use bull-barreled .38 Spl. revolvers with iron sights.

classes for standard revolvers and duty-type semi-automatic pistols. Intended to test shooting skills relevant to the law-enforcement environment, PPC shooting is done at full-size B-27 silhouettes, at ranges from seven to 50 yards. A number of standard courses of fire are used, shot under time limits, and usually requiring shooters to fire from behind barricades in various positions. Target loads in .38 Special or 9mm Para. are favored.

In all practical shooting disciplines, most shooters employ specialized holsters, a matching gun belt, and one or more magazine or speedloader pouches to facilitate reloading.

To contact the sanctioning bodies for the various forms of practical pistol competition, see Appendix B: Information and Training Resources.

Silhouette Competition

In *silhouette shooting,* the targets are life-size or reduced-size steel silhouettes of four game animals--ram, turkey, pig and chicken--that must be knocked over to score a hit. Banks of targets for each animal are set at different distances from the firing line. In some classes of competition, the furthest (ram) targets may be placed as far as 200 meters from the shooter.

Shooting is done from the *standing* position or the *freestyle* position, in which the shooter is positioned on the ground. Competition is held in a variety of classes, for both .22 rimfire and centerfire pistols, with both iron and optical sights, and using standing and freestyle positions. Some shooting classes favor long-barreled .22 target pistols, while others are dominated by typical big-bore hunting revolvers and specialized single-shot pistols in rifle calibers. There is even a class for air pistol shooters.

Handgun silhouette competition utilizes a variety of pistols, fired at ranges as much as 200 yards at full- or reduced-size steel silhouettes of chickens, pigs, turkeys and rams. Most favored are specialized single-shot pistols or single-action revolvers.

Handgun silhouette competitors shoot from the standing position (left), often with highly specialized pistols, or from a variety of freestyle positions, such as shown below.

To contact the sanctioning body for NRA silhouette competition, see Appendix B: Information and Training Resources.

Cowboy Action Competition

Cowboy Action Shooting is a relatively new sport, and reflects a resurgence in interest in the historical American West. Cowboy Action competitors are required to dress in period clothing and assume nicknames reflecting the flavor of the Old West. Most matches have events for pistols, rifles and shotguns.

The single-action revolver is the prototypical pistol for Cowboy Action shooting. Period clothing is a must.

Courses of fire are similar to those used in practical pistol competition, in that they reflect the originality and creativity of the course designer. Thus, the stages at each match are likely to be very different. Extensive

Part of the enjoyment of Cowboy Action competition is dressing in period clothing and gear.

use is made of period props, such as barrels, hay bales, and even small buildings to give the shooter new and interesting challenges. Some pistol events even involve shooting balloons with special shot cartridges while riding a horse. Successful Cowboy Action pistol shooters must be able to fire from a variety of positions, at ranges up to 25 yards, with two hands as well as with just the strong and weak hands.

Targets include metal plates, cardboard silhouettes and the aforementioned balloons. Scoring is calculated on the basis of both the hits achieved and the time taken to complete the stage.

Pistols for Cowboy Action Shooting are limited to those guns (or modern copies) whose designs originated prior to approximately 1900. This generally means a revolver, such as a Colt Peacemaker (or modern copy), Smith & Wesson Schofield or Russian (or modern copy), 1875 Remington (or modern copy) and other similar models.

Cowboy Action shooters have an extensive range of accessories from which to choose, from period clothes, boots and hats to various types of holsters, gun belts, cartridge belts and more.

To contact the sanctioning body for Cowboy Action Shooting see Appendix B: Information and Training Resources.

PERSONAL PROTECTION

Although nearly all of the millions of rounds fired by civilian pistol shooters each year are expended at targets or game, most pistol owners cite "self-defense" among the reasons for owning a gun. The right of self-defense is enshrined in American law, and the majority of states acknowledge the right of law-abiding citizens to carry a firearm for self-protection.

There are generally two situations in which a firearm is used for personal protection: *home defense*, in which the firearm is stored in the home, and *concealed carry*, in which the firearm is carried on the person in public. The requirements of these two types of self-defense are different, and thus usually involve different pistol types and cartridge choices.

In general, any pistol used for self-defense purposes must be able to fire several shots without reloading; and should be reliable, easy to use and easy to reload. Also, it should be chambered for a reasonably powerful cartridge. Semi-automatic pistols and double-action revolvers most closely fit these requirements, and are thus best suited for self-defense use.

The subject of self-defense in or outside the home is far too complex to summarize here. The defensive-minded pistol owner not only must choose among many pistol types, sizes and calibers; he or she must also be proficient in a variety of shooting techniques. Just as importantly, he or she must know techniques for avoiding or evading attacks, the physiological and psychological phenomena that often accompany or follow a violent confrontation, and the mental, legal and social aftermath of using a firearm to protect oneself or one's family. Finally, the pistol owner must also know his or her legal rights and responsibilities regarding self-defense.

Owning a pistol for self-defense is a great responsibility, not to be taken lightly. The proper training will build the knowledge, skills and attitude to use a firearm safely and respon-

Almost any type of pistol can be used for personal protection. Full-size pistols are often used for home defense, while compact models may be preferred for concealed carry.

sibly for self defense. The NRA offers two comprehensive and highly-rated defensive pistol courses: the *Basic Personal Protection In The Home Course,* for pistol owners interested in home defense, and the *Personal Protection Outside The Home Course*, for those wishing to obtain a concealed carry permit. For more information about these courses, call the NRA Education & Training Division, (703) 267-1500.

OPPORTUNITIES FOR SKILL DEVELOPMENT

The NRA Basic Pistol Course should not be regarded as the endpoint of the training experience, but rather as the first step in the development of pistol shooting skills and abilities. There are many ways in which the knowledge, skills and attitude that are acquired in the Basic Pistol Course can be enhanced, from individual practice to formal training and official competition. The selection of the appropriate activity is based on your needs, resources and time schedule.

DRY-FIRE PRACTICE

Dry-fire practice is an inexpensive, safe and time-efficient way to enhance shooting fundamentals and practice the various shooting positions. Dry-firing involves practicing every phase of the firing process using an *unloaded* firearm.

All dry-fire practice must be performed under the following safety rules:
  • The firearm must be completely unloaded
  • All dry-firing is done in a dedicated dry-fire area having a safe backstop at which the gun is pointed
  • No live ammunition is allowed in the dedicated dry-fire area
  • Reloading drills are performed only with dummy ammunition

Of course, even though the firearm is unloaded, it is important to still observe the first Rule for Safe Gun Handling—**ALWAYS** keep the gun pointed in a safe direction.

Dry-firing can be used to practice a variety of skills, including reloading a revolver or semi-automatic pistol; clearing stoppages (using dummy ammunition); practicing various shooting positions (kneeling, squatting, prone, etc.); and, of course, mastering the shooting fundamentals as well as grip, position and NAA (Natural Aiming Area). The ways that dry-firing can be used to enhance shooting skills are limited only by the imagination.

Laser technology affords a variation on traditional dry-fire techniques, in the form of target systems allowing an unmodified firearm to "fire" a beam of laser light at a target sensor. Such systems use a cartridge-shaped laser light inserted into the gun's chamber and activated by the firing pin strike.

LIVE-FIRE PRACTICE

Although dry-fire practice, as well as the review of books, videos and other materials, can add considerably to your knowledge and ability, there is no substitute for live-fire practice in improving pistol shooting skills. Initially, the novice shooter should concentrate upon drills that promote mastery of the shooting fundamentals. Later, as skill improves, more challenging drills may be practiced.

A shooting partner during live-fire exercises not only provides an additional incentive to practice; such a partner can help you better assess your progress. During a live-fire practice session, a partner can observe and give feedback on stance, grip, and shooting fundamentals. On occasion a video record of the practice session may be useful in perfecting form or diagnosing shooting problems, particularly when played back in slow motion. The video camera must always be placed at or behind the firing line, never in front of the muzzle.

WINCHESTER/NRA PISTOL MARKSMANSHIP QUALIFICATION PROGRAM

Any pistol shooter can develop skills and gain recognition for his or her level of proficiency in the Winchester/NRA Pistol Marksmanship Qualification Program, a self-paced recreational shooting activity that provides shooters of all skill levels with both fun and a sense of accomplishment. The Program consists of seven different skill ratings which are earned by attaining the required scores on a series of increasingly challenging courses of fire. For more information on the Winchester/NRA Pistol Marksmanship Qualification Program, see Appendix B: Information and Training Resources.

The Winchester/NRA Pistol Marksmanship Qualification Program offers recognition for increasing levels of shooting skill.

ADDITIONAL TRAINING

The NRA Basic Pistol Course provides a thorough grounding in the fundamentals of safe and effective pistol shooting. Practice and application of these techniques will greatly enhance pistol shooting skill and enjoyment. In recognition of the fact that self-defense is a concern of many pistol owners, the NRA's Education and Training Division offers the NRA Personal Protection In The Home and NRA Personal Protection Outside The Home Courses. These courses cover the essential shooting skills required for effective home defense and concealed carry, and, in terms of the number of shots fired and the diversity of skills taught, are comparable to courses offered at elite shooting schools. In addition to varied shooting and gun handling techniques, these courses also present ways that an armed citizen can avoid, deter, escape or evade a violent confrontation.

Some shooters may wish to avail themselves of non-NRA training available at numerous facilities throughout the country. The instruction provided at such facilities may vary in terms of length, quality, type and cost. Shooters contemplating enrolling at such a facility should consider:
- Reputation of facility
- Geographic location
- Cost of course
- Credentials of instructors
- Student-teacher ratio
- Safety record of institution
- Types of courses offered
- Availability of nearby lodging (for multi-day courses)

Pistol enthusiasts who are primarily interested in improving their skills in a competitive discipline may avail themselves of NRA's Coach Program. This program provides advanced individualized coaching to pistol owners at all levels who are competing in NRA Bullseye, NRA Action Pistol, and NRA Air Pistol matches.

APPENDIXES

APPENDIX A

THE ONE-HANDED SHOOTING POSITION

The well-rounded pistol shooter must be as comfortable with one-handed firing positions as with the more familiar two-handed ones. There are many situations in which one-handed firing may be necessary. Some shooting sports, for example, require a one-handed grip. In some hunting or defensive situations, moreover, a shooter may find it necessary to take a one-handed shot.

The one-handed shooting position taught in this course is the basic position used in NRA bullseye pistol competition. This position is readily adaptable for use in other pistol sports, or in other activities in which one-handed shooting is used.

Assuming the One-Handed Shooting Position

Because the one-handed pistol shooting position offers less support and stability than any of the two-handed positions, good shooting performance in this position is even more reliant upon proper technique.

Perhaps the single most critical factor in one-handed pistol shooting is establishing and using the Natural Aiming Area (NAA). To this end, target shooters, plinkers and others who wish to use any one-handed position should regularly perform the NAA exercise, presented in Chapter 10: Fundamentals of Pistol Shooting Positions.

In the one-handed position, the shooter assumes a stance, with the strong-side (firing) foot forward, the weak-side foot back, and the body facing at an angle from the target. Depending upon body type and proportions, some shooters will end up with the feet aligned directly with the target and the body at roughly a 90-degree angle to the target, while others will position the weak-side foot slightly forward for an "open" stance. The specific foot placement

One-handed standing shooting position.

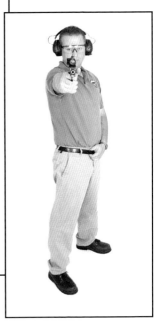

Variations on the one-handed standing shooting position. Left, feet aligned with target; center, extreme open position with feet parallel to target; right, slightly open position favored by many bullseye shooters.

will depend upon the shooter's natural alignment with the target, as revealed by the NAA exercise. Regardless of foot position, the weight should be distributed evenly between the feet, with the knees neither bent nor locked.

The head should be held erect and at an angle that allows the sights to be viewed out of the center of the eye. The strong-side arm and shoulder should be relaxed, with the shoulder in a low position. The firing arm should be bent slightly at the elbow, rather than locked.

When the one-handed position is used for bullseye pistol competition, the non-firing arm is placed in a relaxed position on the waist or in a pants pocket. Many bullseye shooters prefer to rest the hand on the belt buckle, as shown here.

When the one-handed shooting position is used for bullseye target competition, there is no need for the shooter to lean toward the target (as in the isosceles and Weaver positions), as neither of these activities usually requires rapid shooting and recoil control. However, under circumstances in which a heavy-recoiling pistol is used, or during the rapid-fire stage, the shooter's upper body may lean slightly forward, with most of the body weight on the forward (strong-side) leg. The weak-side leg acts as a brace

To assume the standing one-handed shooting position from the low ready position, the pistol is simply raised to eye level, with the final position aligned with the target. If the feet are positioned close together in the low ready position, a small step toward the target may also be necessary.

to support an aggressive, forward-leaning stance, with most of the weight carried on the ball of the strong-side foot.

The one-handed position can easily be assumed from the low ready position, simply by stepping toward the target with the strong-side foot and raising the gun with the strong hand. With practice, the shooter will come to automatically assume the proper foot and body position that is consistent with a proper NAA.

APPENDIX B

INFORMATION AND TRAINING RESOURCES

The following is not meant to be an exhaustive list of the books, magazines, videos and training opportunities available to today's gun owners. Instead, it is only a representative sampling of these resources. Inclusion of a resource in the list below does not imply NRA endorsement of its contents. Consult an NRA Certified Instructor for further information on additional resources that may be available to you.

BOOKS

NRA Firearm Sourcebook. National Rifle Association, Fairfax, VA, 2006. ISBN 0-935998-55-1

Winchester/NRA Marksmanship Qualification Program (booklet). National Rifle Association, Fairfax, VA, 22030.

MAGAZINES

All titles below published monthly by the National Rifle Association of America, Fairfax, VA.

American Rifleman   *InSights*
American Hunter   *Shooting Illustrated*
America's 1st Freedom   *Shooting Sports USA*

VIDEOS/DVDS

Fundamentals of Gun Safety: The Basic Rules of Safe Firearm Ownership. National Rifle Association of America, Fairfax, VA, 1991.

A Woman's Guide to Firearms. Lyon House Productions, Hollywood, CA, 1987.

Personal Protection In The Home. National Rifle Association of America, Fairfax, VA, 2001.

Personal Protection Outside The Home. National Rifle Association of America, Fairfax, VA, 2008.

TRAINING

Consult an NRA Certified Instructor for information on further training opportunities to enhance your knowledge, skills and attitude.

COMPETITION

Shooters wishing to participate in any of the following competitive activities should consult the sanctioning organizations listed for information on rules, equipment and more.

NRA Action Pistol: Competitive Shooting Division, National Rifle Association of America, 11250 Waples Mill Road, Fairfax, VA 22030, (703) 267-1450.

NRA Conventional (Bullseye) Pistol: Competitive Shooting Division, National Rifle Association of America, 11250 Waples Mill Road, Fairfax, VA 22030, (703) 267-1450

NRA Pistol Silhouette, Competitive Shooting Division, National Rifle Association of America, 11250 Waples Mill Road, Fairfax, VA 22030, (703) 267-1450

International Defensive Pistol Association (IDPA): 2232 CR 719, Berryville, AR 72616, (870) 545-3886.

United States Practical Shooting Association/International Practical Shooting Confederation (USPSA/IPSC): P.O. Box 811, 702A Metcalf St., Sedro Wooley, WA 98284, (360) 855-2245.

Cowboy Action Shooting: Single Action Shooting Socieity, 23255 La Palma Ave., Yorba Linda, CA 92887, (714) 694-1800

International Bullseye: ISSF (International Shooting Sports Federation), Bavariaring 21, D-80336 Munchen, Germany, +49 89 544 355 0

APPENDIX C

FACTS ABOUT THE NRA

Established in 1871, the National Rifle Association of America (NRA) is a non-profit organization supported entirely by membership fees and by donations from public-spirited citizens.

The NRA does not receive any appropriations from Congress, nor is it a trade organization. It is not affiliated with any gun or ammunition manufacturers, or with any businesses which deal in guns or ammunition.

The membership roster of the NRA has included seven Presidents of the United States, two Supreme Court Chief Justices of the United States, and many of America's outstanding diplomats, military leaders, members of Congress, and other public officials.

Originally formed to promote marksmanship training, the NRA has since reached out to establish a wide variety of activities, ranging from gun safety

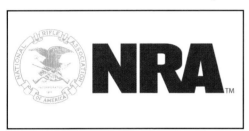

programs for children and adults to gun collecting and gunsmithing.

Law enforcement personnel throughout the country have also received training from NRA Certified Law Enforcement Instructors in the firearm skills needed to protect themselves and the public.

In addition, clubs that are enrolled or affiliated with the NRA exist in communities across the nation, teaching youths and adults gun safety, marksmanship, and responsibility while also providing recreational activities.

The NRA cooperates with federal agencies, all branches of the U.S. Armed Forces, and state and local governments that are interested in training and safety programs.

The basic goals of the NRA are to:
- Protect and defend the Constitution of the United States, especially in regard to the Second Amendment right of the individual citizen to keep and bear arms.
- Promote public safety, law and order, and the national defense.
- Train citizens and members of law enforcement agencies and the armed forces in the safe handling and efficient use of firearms.
- Foster and promote the shooting sports at local, state, regional, national, and international levels.
- Promote hunter safety and proper wildlife management.

For additional information about the NRA, including programs, publications and membership, contact: National Rifle Association of America, 11250 Waples Mill Road, Fairfax, VA 22030, (800) NRA-3888, www.nra.org.

To contact the NRA for assistance or additional information, please direct all inquiries to:
National Rifle Association of America
11250 Waples Mill Road
Fairfax, VA 22030
(703) 267-1000 (Main Switchboard)
NRA.org

Members' Insurance
Life, Accident, & Health
(800) 247-7989

Property & Liability Insurance
Lockton Risk Services
Arms Care Plus
Excess Personal Liability
Firearms Instructors
Self-Defense
Club Property & Liability
Business Owner's Insurance
(877) 487-5407

NRA Program Materials Center
(800) 336-7402
Order on-line at: http://materials.nrahq.org

Technical Questions
Receiving answers to technical questions is a privilege reserved for NRA members. (A non-member may submit a question if the inquiry is accompanied by a membership application.) Each question must be in the form of a letter addressed to:

> **Dope Bag**
> NRA Publications
> 11250 Waples Mill Road
> Fairfax, VA 22030

Each inquiry must contain the individual's NRA membership identification number. Inquiries must be limited to one specific question per letter. Questions regarding the value of any type of firearm will not be accepted. In addition, each inquiry must include a stamped, self-addressed, legal-size envelope. No technical questions will be answered by telephone, e-mail or fax.

APPENDIX D

POPULAR PISTOL CARTRIDGES

RIMFIRE CARTRIDGES

.22 Long Rifle—One of the most popular cartridges made for pistols and rifles. Because of its low recoil, noise and cost, it is an excellent cartridge to use when learning how to shoot. Probably the most popular match cartridge in existence, it can also be used to hunt small game.

.22 Winchester Magnum—Introduced in 1959 by Winchester, it is an elongated and powerful .22 rimfire cartridge. It can be used for hunting small game.

CENTERFIRE CARTRIDGES

.25 ACP—Known in Europe at the 6.35mm Browning, this cartridge was introduced in 1902 in conjunction with a small Colt semi-automatic pistol. It is the smallest commercially produced center-fire pistol cartridge. Many small pocket pistols are chambered for the .25 ACP.

.32 ACP—Commonly known in Europe as the 7.65mm Browning, this cartridge was introduced in 1899 for use in the Browning-designed autoloading pocket pistol manufactured by Fabrique Nationale in Belgium. This cartridge is mainly used in small pocket pistols.

.380 ACP—Also known as the .380 Auto, 9mm Browning Short, 9mm Kurz and 9mm Corto. Introduced about 1912 for a Browning-designed autoloading pistol manufactured by Fabrique Nationale in Belgium. Although used in many small semi-automatic pistols, this cartridge also has many large semi-automatic models chambered for it, and has been used by uniformed police in Europe.

9mm Luger (Parabellum, 9x19)—This cartridge was introduced in 1902 for the Luger pistol. The 9mm Luger/Parabellum is one of the most popular pistol cartridges used today. It is used by the U.S. military and by NATO allies.

.38 Super Colt Automatic—Introduced in 1929 by Colt, the .38 Super is a more powerful version of the .38 ACP cartridge. Dimensionally the same as the .38 ACP but loaded to higher pressures, the .38 Super should not be fired in guns intended only for .38 ACP cartridges.

.38 Special—Introduced by Smith & Weson about 1902. One of the most popular revolver cartridges made. Police officers around the country have traditionally carried .38 Special revolvers. This cartridge is available in standard pressure loadings, and in + P and + P + loadings. However, before using + P or + P + cartridges in a pistol, be sure that it is approved for such use.

.357 Magnum—Introduced by Smith & Wesson in 1935. More powerful than the .38 Special, the .357 Magnum is based on the .38 Special cartridge case lengthened by about 1/10th of an inch.

10mm Auto—Designed in early 1980s for the Dornaus and Dixon Bren Ten pistol, the 10mm Auto cartridge has gained in popularity. Today, a number of manufacturers make pistols that are chambered for it. More powerful than the .357 Magnum, the 10mm Auto cartridge brings magnum power to average-sized semi-automatic pistols.

.40 S&W—Introduced commercially about 1990 for use in semi-automatic pistols. The .40 S&W is a shorter version of the 10mm Auto cartridge, and produces less recoil and muzzle blast. However, for self-defense purposes, the cartridge still has very good kinetic energy.

.41 Magnum—Introduced by Remington in 1964 for the Smith & Wesson Model 57 revolver. The .41 Magnum and the .44 Magnum. However, the .41 Magnum has not achieve the popularity of that cartridge.

.44 Special—Introduced in 1907 by Smith & Wesson, this cartridge was designed to be more powerful than the .44 S&W Russian cartridge (which was originally loaded with blackpowder).

.44 Magnum—Introduced by Remington for Smith & Wesson in 1956. This cartridge was the most powerful standard handgun cartridge at that time. It is used in hunting medium sized game at close ranges.

.45 ACP—Delevoped by John Browning in 1905, and adopted as the U.S. military pistol cartridge from 1911 to the late 1980s. This cartridge is currently used in conventional and other types of pistol shooting competitions.

.45 Colt—Also incorrectly referred to as the .45 Long Colt. Introduced in 1873 as a blackpowder cartridge for the famous Colt *Peacemaker* single-action revolver. Today, the .45 Colt is loaded with modern smokeless powder by many ammunition companies, and a number of gun manufacturers currently produce revolvers that are chambered for this powerful cartridge. (Early-model Colt revolvers with serial numbers 160,000 and below were made during the era of black powder. Such revolvers should not be fired with smokeless powder ammunition.)

GLOSSARY

ACP: An abbreviation for Automatic Colt Pisol. Used in conjunction with caliber designations. Example: a .45 ACP cartridge.

Action: A series of moving parts that allow a firearm to be loaded, fired, and unloaded.

Backstrap: The rear, vertical portion of the pistol frame that lies between the grip panels.

Bore: The inside of the barrel of a firearm.

Caliber: The diameter of a projectile or the distance between the lands in the bore of a firearm.

Cartridge: A complete single unit of ammunition including the projectile, case, primer, and powder charge.

Centerfire: A type of cartridge which has the primer centrally located in the base of the case.

Chamber: The part of a firearm in which a cartridge is contained at the instant of firing.

Cylinder: The part of a revolver that holds ammunition in individual chambers that are rotated into firing position by the action of the trigger or hammer.

Double-action: A type of pistol action in which squeezing the trigger will both cock and release the hammer or internal firing mechanism.

Dry firing: The shooting of an unloaded gun.

Ejector: The part of a pistol which ejects an empty cartridge case or a cartridge from the gun.

Grooves: The shallow, spiral cuts in a bore that together with the lands make up the rifling in the bore of a barrel.

Hammer: The part of a pistol that pivots on an axis at the rear of the frame, and, when activated by the trigger, causes the firing pin to strike a cartridge.

Hangfire: A perceptible delay in the ignition of a cartridge after the primer has been struck by the firing pin.

Misfire: A failure of a cartridge to fire after the primer has been struck by the firing pin.

Muzzle: The front end of the barrel from which a projectile exits.

Parabellum: Taken from Latin, this term translates as "prepare for war." During World War 1, the Deutsche Waffen und Munitionsfabrik (DWM) used this term for its Luger pistol and a machine gun. Parabellum is used today as a synonym for Luger to identify 7.65mm and 9mm Luger ammunition.

Patridge sight: A type of sight designed by E.E. Patridge in the late 1800's, generally used on handguns. It has a rear sight with a square notch, and a front sight consisting of a thick blade that is flat on top.

Pistol: A gun that has a short barrel and can be held, aimed, fired with one hand.

+P (Plus P): Cartridges which are loaded to higher pressures than standard ammunition.

+P+ (Plus P Plus): Cartridges which are loaded to higher pressures than +P ammunition.

Plinking: Informal shooting at a variety of targets.

Revolver: A pistol that has a rotating cylinder containing a number of firing chambers. The action of the trigger or hammer will line up a chamber with the barrel and firing pin.

Rifling: Spiral lands and grooves in the barrel bore that provide a stabilizing spin to a bullet so that it will be more accurate in flght.

Rimfire: A cartridge which has the chemical compound of the primer located inside the rim of the case.

Round: Another term for a cartridge.

Semi-automatic: A pistol that fires a single cartridge each time the trigger is pulled, and which automatically extracts and ejects the empty case and inserts a new cartridge into the chamber.

Single-action: A type of pistol action in which pulling the trigger will release the hammer.

Sights: Mechanical, optical, or electronic devices used to aim a pistol.

Squib load: A cartridge which develops less than normal pressure or velocity after ignition of the cartridge.

INDEX